W9-ABN-288

TOM JONES

Adventure and Providence

TWAYNE'S MASTERWORK STUDIES

Robert Lecker, *General Editor*

TOM JONES

Adventure and Providence

PATRICK REILLY

Twayne Publishers • Boston

A DIVISION OF G. K. HALL & CO.

Tom Jones: Adventure and Providence
Patrick Reilly

Twayne's Masterwork Studies No. 72
Copyright 1991 by G. K. Hall & Co.
All rights reserved.
Published by Twayne Publishers
A division of G. K. Hall & Co.
70 Lincoln Street
Boston, Massachusetts 02111

Copyediting supervised by Barbara Sutton.
Book production by Gabrielle B. McDonald.
Typeset in Sabon with Bembo display type by Compset, Inc.
of Beverly, Massachusetts.

First published 1991.
10 9 8 7 6 5 4 3 2 1 (HC)
10 9 8 7 6 5 4 3 2 1 (PB)

The paper used in this publication meets the minimum requirements
of American National Standard for Information Sciences—Permanence
of Paper for Printed Library Materials, ANSI Z39.48-1984. ∞™

Printed and bound in the United States of America.

Library of Congress Cataloging-in-Publication Data

Reilly, Patrick.
    Tom Jones : adventure and providence / Patrick Reilly.
        p.   cm.—(Twayne's masterwork studies ; no. 72)
    Includes bibliographical references and index.
    ISBN 0-8057-9422-0 (hc : alk. paper).—ISBN 0-8057-8143-9 (pbk :
alk. paper)
    1. Fielding, Henry, 1707–1754. History of Tom Jones.   I. Title.
II. Series.
PR3454.H7R4   1991
823′.5—dc20
                                                           90-22099
                                                              CIP

For Philip and Rosemary Hobsbaum

Surely a man may speak truth with a smiling countenance.

> —Henry Fielding

no man enjoy'd life more than he did, tho' few had less reason to do so.

> —Lady Mary Wortley Montagu

Contents

Note on the References and Acknowledgments

Page references (in parentheses) are to the single-volume Penguin edition of *Tom Jones* (Middlesex, England: Penguin, 1966), edited by R. P. C. Mutter. I am grateful to Penguin for permission to quote from this text and from *Henry Fielding: A Critical Anthology*, edited by C. J. Rawson. I am also grateful to Gale Research Company, Detroit, for permission to quote from *Literary Criticism from 1400 to 1800*, edited by Dennis Poupard and Mark W. Scott. The best, most modern, and most scholarly edition is the two-volume Wesleyan Edition, *The History of Tom Jones, a Foundling* (Oxford: Clarendon Press, 1974), edited by Fredson Bowers with an introduction and commentary by Martin C. Battestin. Among the cheaper reprints available is the two-volume Everyman Library edition (London: Dent; New York: Dutton, 1963) with an introduction by A. R. Humphreys.

My preeminent obligation is to my wife, Rose, for her patience and skill in preparing the manuscript for publication. I am also indebted to my daughter, Patricia, for her assistance in the final stages of typing the book.

Chronology: Henry Fielding's Life and Works

1707	Henry Fielding born 22 April at Sharpham Park in Somerset to a family with aristocratic connections.
1719–1724	Attends Eton.
1724–1728	Man about London.
1728	First poem, *The Masquerade*, published, and first play, *Love in Several Masques*, produced and published.
1728–1729	Studies law at the University of Leyden.
1730–1737	Writes more than twenty comedies and burlesques, including *The Temple Beau* (1730); *The Author's Farce* (1730); *Rape upon Rape* (1730); *The Tragedy of Tragedies* (1731); *The Grub-Street Opera* (1731); *The Lottery* (1732); *The Covent-Garden Tragedy* (1732); *The Mock Doctor* (1732) and *The Miser* (1733), both adapted from Molière; *Don Quixote in England* (1734); *Pasquin* (1736); *Eurydice* (1737); *The Historical Register for 1736* (1737), and *Eurydice Hiss'd* (1737).
1734	Marries Charlotte Cradock, the inspiration for his later heroines Sophia Western and Amelia.
1736	Fielding's first child, Charlotte, born.
1737	Stage Licensing Act comes into force and ends Fielding's career as a dramatist. Fielding's second child, Harriet, born. Fielding admitted as a law student at the Middle Temple.
1739–1741	Edits *The Champion*, an Opposition paper, containing also essays by Fielding of a general, nonpolitical nature.
1740	Is called to the Bar. Richardson's novel *Pamela* is published.
1741	Anonymously publishes *An Apology for the Life of Mrs. Shamela Andrews*, a parody of *Pamela*.
1742	Fall of Sir Robert Walpole. Fielding publishes his first novel,

The History of the Adventures of Joseph Andrews, and of His Friend Mr. Abraham Adams, Written in Imitation of the Manner of Cervantes. Daughter Charlotte dies.

1743   Publishes three volumes of *Miscellanies*, containing poems, plays, and essays (including the *Essay on Conversation* and the *Essay on the Knowledge of the Characters of Men*); *A Journey from This World to the Next*, an otherworldly fiction modeled on Lucian; and the novel *The Life of Mr. Jonathan Wild the Great.*

1744   Sister Sarah Fielding publishes her novel *David Simple;* Fielding writes the preface to the second edition. Wife Charlotte dies.

1745   Charles Edward Stuart, the Young Pretender, lands in Scotland in July and reaches Derby in December.

1745–1746   Fielding edits *The True Patriot,* supporting the Hanoverian cause against the Jacobites. (The main action of *Tom Jones* occurs during the 1745 Jacobite Rebellion).

1746   Charles Edward is defeated at Culloden in April.

1747   Provides the preface and contributions to Sarah Fielding's *Familiar Letters.* Marries Mary Daniel, his housekeeper and formerly his first wife's maid.

1747–1748   Edits *The Jacobite's Journal,* in the Hanoverian cause.

1748   Birth of son William. Congratulates Richardson on the publication of *Clarissa,* a novel he admires. Becomes justice of the peace for Westminster (his jurisdiction is later extended to the whole of Middlesex). Daughter Mary Amelia born.

1749   Publishes *The History of Tom Jones, a Foundling* on 28 February. Delivers *Charge to the Grand Jury.*

1750   Daughter Sophia born.

1751   Publishes *An Enquiry into the Causes of the Late Increase of Robbers, etc., with Some Proposals for Remedying This Growing Evil,* an important legal-sociological work, and in December his last novel, *Amelia.*

1752   Edits *The Covent-Garden Journal.* Daughter Louisa born.

1753   Publishes *A Proposal for Making an Effectual Provision for the Poor, for Amending Their Morals, and for Rendering Them Useful Members of the Society,* another legal-sociological work. Is directed by the Duke of Newcastle to draw up a plan for suppressing crime.

1754   Publishes a revised edition of *Jonathan Wild.* His last child,

Chronology

Allen, is born. Fielding, very ill, resigns his office as Bow Street magistrate and leaves for Lisbon. Dies near Lisbon on 8 October.

1755   *The Journal of a Voyage to Lisbon* is published posthumously in February and, in a more authentic text, in December.

Literary and Historical Context

I

The Rivalries of Art

There are certain names we cannot speak or even think of without simultaneously summoning a companion: Romulus and Remus, Cain and Abel, Barnum and Bailey. Richardson and Fielding provide perhaps the most striking example from literature of this twinship and reciprocity. The interaction between these two careers is so remarkable as to suggest the design of art rather than the randomness of life; it is impossible to discuss the one without recourse to the other. *Joseph Andrews* is a direct response to *Pamela*. There follows a long, shared silence as the collaborative competitors create their respective masterpieces (1742–48). (True, Fielding published three volumes of *Miscellanies* in 1743 and also *Jonathan Wild*, but the latter was probably begun in 1740). Within an interval of a few months, *Tom Jones* succeeds *Clarissa*. Two years later Fielding gets in first with *Amelia*, to be almost instantly countered by *The History of Sir Charles Grandison*. The six great novels go in pairs, symmetry perfected by the fact that Fielding's opening two male portraits are balanced by his rival's opening two female portraits, while Fielding's concluding female portrait is complemented by Richardson's switch to a male hero. There is pattern here rather than coincidence, a self-definition made sharper by the challenge of the adversary. In these contrasting works two types of genius, two conceptions of art, two techniques, two moral ideals, and two conflicting temperaments confront one another. Nowhere is this opposition clearer than in the clash of the two masterpieces, *Tom Jones* and *Clarissa*. Despite his generous admiration for *Clarissa* (in sharp contrast to his disdain for *Pamela*), Fielding is still criticizing Richardson in *Tom Jones*, though more obliquely, more positively and more artistically than he did in *Shamela* or *Joseph Andrews*. More precisely, Richardson is the symbol and cultural chieftain of different groups of enemies, Pharisees all, whom Fielding seeks to expose.

If the degree of interaction between the careers is surprising, the adversarial reciprocity and counterstimulation of the novels are wholly predictable. New literary genres are continually formed from existing ones. We should have difficulty in understanding any book that bore no family resemblance to any other. In taking our bearings from the known, we establish a norm enabling us to discriminate between what is familiar and what is original in the new work. This relationship, stronger within specific genres, is strongest of all within the genre of the novel. Novels necessarily feed upon previous novels; they find their sustenance, their means of survival, in preceding fictions. A new novelist's task is always the correction of obsolete or misleading versions of reality imposed by earlier novels; any significant novel is an antinovel.[1] Cervantes, the great progenitor, exposing the absurdities of romance, creates *Don Quixote,* and his superb anticreation becomes the model and standard for all succeeding fictions. Nearly all fiction of any real quality, as the history of the novel makes plain, reacts against the fallacious fiction of its past: Cervantes against romance, Fielding against Richardson, Thackeray against the "Silver Fork" school, Virginia Woolf against the late realists, the *nouveau roman* against a spurious solidarity between man and things.

It should not surprise us, then, that Fielding, seeking a new career after the Licensing Act abruptly ended his theater vocation—that choice, as he said, between a hackney writer and a hackney coachman[2]—should have found in Richardson the incentive to compose his own fiction through ridiculing the faults of his predecessor.

That, after all, is the routine way in which the novel evolves and "progresses" as a literary form. The best criticism of a work of art is an answering, a countervailing work of art, as *Portrait of a Lady* replies to *Middlemarch,* or *The Fall* to *Les Misérables,* or *Lord of the Flies* to *The Coral Island.* Fielding's fiction is a critique in action of Richardson, in which he subjects, through his own achievement, the achievement of his rival to the most stringent analysis and assessment. Richardson, for his part, was confirmed in the superiority of his own art by contrasting it with what he could only regard as the corrupt art of Fielding: "But in an age so dissolute as the present, what can be said for the morality (for the morality shall I say?) propagated in *Tom Jones?*"[3] In such fructifying enmity *Clarissa* and *Tom Jones* come to live in and against each other.

This mutually fertilizing hostility had begun in 1740 with the publication of *Pamela* and the ensuing epidemical frenzy of adulation; the whole country seemed ravished by the book, with the clergy leading the chorus of praise for its moral purity. Pope declared that it would do more good than all the volumes of sermons published in recent years. Fielding, torn between amusement and indignation, was stung into exposing what he regarded as a morally contemptible and technically incompetent work. His immediate response was the parody *Shamela* (1741), brilliant and bawdy but necessarily restricted by virtue of its negative, purely destructive conception. In 1742 he published *Joseph Andrews* as a more pondered refutation of Richardson, for the first time advancing his own opposing idea of art and the rationale of the novel.

Joseph Andrews also starts life as an anti-Richardson joke, a parodic demolition of Richardson's much-feted novel. A young woman battling with a would-be rapist to preserve her honor is not funny—but Fielding suspected hypocrisy in the handling of the theme. For him, Pamela is a fraud, a commercial adventuress taking high risks in the hope of a high return. She wants and finally obtains marriage to her assailant, risking violation in the process. We may admire her as an intrepid gambler who brings it off, but *not* as a model of female virtue, for she is schemer rather than saint, artful rather than innocent, and it is the element of calculating self-interest in her behavior (paradoxically concealed from herself as from her creator) that so offends Fielding.[4]

Fielding's opening chapters reveal a young man, Pamela's brother Joseph (the name is chosen with the heroic Old Testament resister of Potiphar's wife in mind), battling to defend *his* honor against the lustful sister of Richardson's randy squire—for Fielding, an inherently comic situation in that all probability and physiology are against the rape of a man by a woman. But it is with the entry of Abraham Adams, that other biblical namesake, that Fielding's creative imagination truly takes fire, and the result is Fielding's first great novel of the road with its panoramic survey of English society in the eighteenth century. The patriarchal Adams, a pilgrim like his great forerunner, rapidly takes over as presiding character, and comedy flows from his encounters with people of all vocations and classes as he travels through England on a journey back from urban corruption to rural innocence. This new, enlarged world, expansive and open, is in itself a critique, enacted in art, of what, for Fielding, was the stiflingly suffocating world of Richardson's imagination. *Pamela*, the much-lauded moral exemplum, was, in Fielding's view, actually a rather vulgar bourgeois success story, in which the sprawling, diversified life of eighteenth-century civilization is attenuated to a scheming minx, a silly squire, and a clutch of servants. It was, in every sense, for Fielding, a shrunken and shriveled world in which the single question of female chastity had crowded out every other human concern. Fielding presents his own panoramic largesse as an antidote to this egotistic reductionism, and his prayer to Experience, petitioning an acquaintance with "every kind of character, from the minister at his levee, to the bailiff in his spunging-house; from the duchess at her drum, to the landlady behind her bar" (609), shows that he both knew and relished his superiority to Richardson in this regard. The world is bigger, more vibrant and fecund, than Richardson's obsessive narrowness allows. Take yourself seriously, exhorts Richardson, for nothing is more serious than the self: *I* care for myself, says Jane Eyre, that sister of Pamela, at a moment of high temptation.[5] Do not take yourself so seriously, retorts Fielding: the self is only a small part of a much greater whole.

The fullness of Fielding confronts Richardsonian restriction. Fielding brings to the contest his own male fairy tale of the young hero, outmatched and disadvantaged, who nevertheless captures the king's daughter and the king's fortune, golden girl and golden mountain, to match Richardson's female fairy tale of the pent-up Beauty, enduring her trials, to be rewarded when the Beast, tamed by her goodness, is finally transformed into Prince Charming. After the negative success of *Shamela* and the qualified triumph of *Joseph Andrews*, Fielding carries his critique of Richardson's vision to its superb apotheosis in *Tom Jones*. To anyone still doubtful of the positive values, the ideal, underlying Fielding's mockery of his rival, *Tom Jones* supplies the triumphant answer.

F. R. Leavis dismisses *Tom Jones* as a work of crude, external action, manifestly inferior to the Richardsonian novel that focuses on the subtle, inner life of its characters.[6] But Fielding is a comedian who proposes a walk round the building, not an investigation of the cellar—there will be no journeys to the interior, no searchings for hearts of darkness, in his fiction. The aim is to let in fresh air, to lead us out of Richardson's fetid, dark corners into the openness of the landscape, away from self-obsession to the ampleness of the world, God's plenty.

The challenge to Richardson had the splendid consequence of originating two very different traditions of the novel in English: the psychological novel, intense, introspective, individualistic; and the social novel, freewheeling, extrovert, panoramic. Those who prefer Richardson's murky depths are free to indulge their fascination. What they may not do is devalue the other tradition or slight Fielding's major contribution to the development of English fiction. It is not simply that Fielding is the ancestor of Dickens, though that in itself should command respect and admiration. Those who know Joyce will recognize how beholden *Ulysses* is not only to the author of *Clarissa* but just as significantly to the author of *Tom Jones*. To have some claim in the paternity of such undisputed masters as Dickens and Joyce is a prima facie case for a parallel recognition. The prime aim of this study will be to exhibit *Tom Jones* as the masterwork of a master novelist.

2

The Importance of the Work

E. M. Forster supplies a cynical explanation for our readiness to applaud the class of book to which *Tom Jones* belongs: "One always tends to overpraise a long book because one has got through it."[1] Fielding, with his gift for self-mockery, might have smiled approvingly. But however charming in the creator, such self-deprecating good humor would be inappropriate in the critic of *Tom Jones*. There are irrefutably excellent reasons for celebrating *Tom Jones,* apart from its length and our sense of self-congratulation in having traversed it.

The importance of the work has, if anything, been enhanced by recent developments in literary criticism and cultural history. The acknowledgment of its historical importance, its significance in terms of what Matthew Arnold calls the historical estimate, are, of course, undeniable, conceded even by Fielding's detractors. Leavis, magisterially dismissing *Tom Jones* as lacking subtlety of matter and organization, as too simple for mature people—"life isn't long enough to permit one's giving much time to Fielding"[2]—nevertheless admits Fielding's importance as begetter of the new genre that was destined to become the exemplary literary object, displacing poem and play as the type of literary experience: "to say that the English novel began with him is as reasonable as such propositions ever are." It is, however grudged, a crucial admission. To be the literary parent of Jane Austen, Dickens, George Eliot, Hardy, Lawrence, Conrad, and Joyce is no trifle, to be casually recorded and filed away.

In addition, the text is of prime importance in illustrating a great revolution in ethical thought. At certain historical moments, watersheds in the development of civilized sensibility, it is possible to observe the moral life revising itself, either by reducing the emphasis it had formerly placed upon certain elements, characteristics, and attributes, or by promoting new or previously underrated values to a position of preeminence in the reconstituted scheme.[3] Sometimes the change, the reallocation of values, is revolutionary, a large-scale transfer of loyalties from one concept of virtue to another, from one mode of organizing the moral life to a radically different or even antithetical mode. Such a revolutionary reordering occurred in the first half of the eighteenth century, and *Tom Jones* is one of the chief cultural markers of this upheaval.

If Vico is right in asserting that each culture expresses its own collective experience, we may conclude that the Enlightenment was distinguished by its hostility to the view of man expressed theologically by Calvin and psychologically by Hobbes, the view that defined him either as a sink of iniquity or as an inescapably selfish, aggressive, mistrusting animal.[4] Shaftesbury, so crucial as a shaper of the new sensibility, attacked the Church for its emphasis on original sin; in its anxiety to convince men of sin, the Church had become the foe of virtue. The older, seventeenth-century view of man, whether Hobbesian or Augustinian, was a calumny; on this, whatever their other differences, the men of the new age were unanimous. A revolution in ethical thought had taken place, and *Tom Jones* is a prime exhibit of the new benevolist mentality.

In the preface to *Jonathan Wild,* Fielding repudiates the view that Newgate is simply human nature with the mask off; the idea of a universal Yahoodom is for him a slander on man.[5] Tom Jones attacks the Old Man of the Hill for his pessimistic view of human nature, and his misanthropic devaluation of life—"the silly business of the world"

(431)—is irreconcilable with Fielding's celebration of life as joyful adventure. Even the paragon Amelia is rebuked by Dr. Harrison for her despairing blanket condemnation of human beings in Gulliver's fashion.[6] In the hero of *Tom Jones* Fielding shows us the good man of the new benevolist ethic, feeling delight in the happiness he brings to others and pitying the wretch who has never savored the pleasures of altruism and compassion (638).[7]

Of course, the greatness of *Tom Jones* transcends its historical interest as either pioneering novel or cultural marker; Fielding has today become our contemporary, as fiction conspicuously grows more provisional, more anxiously self-questioning and self-reflective. Modern critics increasingly question the axioms of nineteenth-century realism that the novel is essentially about plot, character, description, and recognize instead that it is also about structure, pattern, form—less a representation than a making of life. Richardson, the great early master of representational realism, is deservedly praised for persuading the reader that what he experiences when reading is as real as what he experiences in the ordinary transactions of life. Fielding, by contrast, stresses the play aspect of art, overtly calling attention to himself as game-player or impresario, displaying for all to see the "lie" he has made, the fictionality he commands, inviting the reader into the novel in novel ways. Today, with the new emphasis on fabulation, the call for a more verbal kind of fiction, a less realistic but more artistic kind of narrative, the architectonic novel that Fielding pioneered with *Tom Jones* seems more relevant than the realistic achievement of Richardson.

Yet Fielding still awaits the recognition he deserves. He is one of those writers (Jane Austen is another) for whom the onslaughts of enemies are sometimes less damaging than the testimonials of friends. In an otherwise unexceptionable defense of Fielding, Middleton Murry says this: "One may admit, without any reluctance, that Fielding's sense of form is, by the standards of subsequent achievement, defective. His prefaces, his long interludes, and his innumerable minor digressions would be better out of the way" (*Lit. Crit.*, 242). Could misjudgment be greater? Form is precisely Fielding's triumph, his subject matter superbly embodied in the achieved content which is art. Technique is not some secondary thing, some external contrivance or mechanical affair (in Fielding's case, so goes the indictment, a *very* mechanical affair), but a deep and primary operation, a passionate private vision finding objectification in exacting technical search. There is no greater mistake than to regard Fielding as an oafish, overbearing extrovert who insists upon managing both his reader and his characters. "Fielding" is an artful device of Fielding; even when the "I" thus created is ostensibly the author himself, we can always distinguish between the narrator and the author who presents him. The authorial commentary that Murry deplores furnishes a moral world encompassing the characters, supplying a wisdom that no character can command, and exhibiting a temperament that always exists in a context of ironic play. Without the narrator *Tom Jones* would still be a good read; with him it is a great novel, a great comedy.

To enlighten the foolish without destroying them, to present an image of life triumphing over chance: such have always been the aims of comedy, "pure" comedy, as distinct from the corrective, satirical comedy of Ben Jonson. The essence of Fielding's comedy is that it embodies in symbolic form our sense of joy in feeling that we can meet and master the changes and chances of life as it confronts us. In comedy the norm is not morality but deliverance; it minimizes the seriousness of the situations in which its characters become involved and nearly always finds some means of reassuring the reader. Any attentive reader of *Tom Jones knows* in the incest episode that a mistake has been made and waits easily, unanxiously, to see it detected—we sympathize but never suffer with the hero. Those critics who seem curiously aggrieved because Tom has *not* slept with his mother exhibit at once a strange itch for the perverse and an incapacity for providential comedy. And it is the unjustly criticized form of his book that distinguishes Fielding as the great master and founder of the providentially comic novel. It is not an achievement that we, in our dark, despondent age, should lightly disparage or patronize.

His severest critic, Samuel Johnson, should, of all men, have recognized the triumph of Fielding's art. "If the world be promiscuously described, I cannot see of what use it can be to read the account; or why it may not be as safe to turn the eye immediately upon mankind, as upon a mirror which shows all that presents itself without discrimination."[8] Yet the multifarious, miscellaneous world presses on us, and nowhere more importunately than in the novel, with its voracious appetite for fact, its indiscriminate rage for reality, its dangerous fidelity to data. The risk of the novel, in its commitment to formal realism, is that it may succumb to a welter of detail, be submerged in the randomness of the real, fall into incoherence as it seeks to reproduce the external world. Defoe's capitulation to data reveals what happens in the absence of artistic control and a selective, discriminating intelligence. Fielding, continuously aware of the status of his novels as artifacts, as form imposed on the flux of reality, as a second creation, shows, contrastingly, how the world is to be mastered by and in art. The data of reality lack the intrinsic structure that has been identified from Aristotle onward as the essential element of a work of art. To resist the overwhelming miscellany of the world: this, as Dr. Johnson saw from the start, would be the major problem confronting the new genre. Both in style and content Fielding triumphs over the world; he satisfies our hunger for the meaningful ordering of experience without denying our empirical observation of its randomness and particularity. With Fielding the novel becomes a more conscious and purposive art. Form in literature is an arousing and fulfilling of desire, leading us to anticipate and be gratified by its sequence. *Tom Jones,* through its form, consummately satisfies the desires it arouses. That is what the rest of this book will seek to demonstrate.

3

Critical Reception

Fielding and Richardson. They go on slugging it out like two heavy-weights, with the different historical periods reflecting the shifting fortunes of the fight. Richardson clearly took the eighteenth century; he had, surprisingly, the great Johnson in his corner, though one might have thought it safe to predict that the mandarin of neoclassicism, the creator of Imlac, would have preferred the generalizing Fielding to his minutely particularizing rival.[1] And he had the fulsomely ecstatic Diderot: "I will sell my books . . . but thou, Richardson, shalt remain with me on the same shelf as Moses, Homer, Euripides and Sophocles."[2] The mood of determined sensibility may seem a trifle excessive, but, allowing for the willed exaggeration, it is the verdict of the eighteenth century, from ordinary clergyman to the Marquis de Sade, concerning the unquestioned superiority of the author of *Clarissa* to the author of *Tom Jones.*

Fielding recovers to take the nineteenth century on points, with the eulogistic Coleridge serving, at the very least, as a counterbalance to Johnson.[3] Most of the leading Romantics—Scott, Hazlitt, Byron—find much to admire in Fielding, little in his adversary. As the century advances, Fielding still commands the greater critical attention both at home and abroad (Thackeray, Hippolyte Taine), and, toward its close, Henry James, perhaps as surprising a celebrant as Johnson is a censurer, praises the fine intelligence of the narrator of *Tom Jones,* necessary complement to the robust animal health of its hero, thereby adumbrating the two-plot theory developed in our own day.[4] Even Fielding's opponents—Ford Madox Ford is the most virulent—condemn him in the light of alleged advances in narrative technique that have evolved since he wrote rather than as the inferior of Richardson (Rawson, 353–66).

In our own century Richardson has made something of a comeback, with some distinguished backers (Frank Kermode, Ian Watt, Angus Wilson) supporting his cause; Wilson in fact ranks *Clarissa* among the world's finest novels, not only for its pioneer psychological perception, but for its consummate organization as a work of art. But neither has Fielding lacked his eminent advocates, among whom can be counted Middleton Murry, William Empson, and André Gide. Assessing the academic criticism of the twentieth century, we might fairly conclude that Fielding just shades it, aided, no doubt, by increased interest in theories of fiction (fabulation, structure, form, play) that find more to sustain them in Fielding's freewheeling art than in Richardson's detailed realism. Nevertheless, as the conclusion of this chapter will show, the contest is not yet over and is forever liable to be resurrected in some new controversy, some unanticipated area of concern, flaring up in circumstances that might well have surprised the age-old competitors.

What soon impresses any student of the critical debate concerning *Tom Jones* is the startlingly contradictory nature of the judgments expressed, the starkly uncompromising status of the disagreements. The divergence is not of the type that results when one set of critics find faults outweighing merits while their opponents tip the scales in the contrary direction, with everything depending at last on a variation in emphasis. Here disagreement is total and unappeasable: what the detractors deplore is, arrestingly, what the celebrants extol, what disgusts some delights others, and the same features are reviled or revered according to the perspective taken. This is as true in discrete particular as in general assay.

Consider, for example, Taine's rebuke to Fielding for his vulgarity—no less severe for coming, perhaps inconsistently, from someone who tells man that he must cease to regard himself as the last of angels and recognize himself as the first of animals. (Fielding, so committed to earth, might easily be cited as the writer who best exemplifies the exhortation). What especially upsets Taine is Fielding's alleged disregard for the modesty of his heroines, the distressing fact that "wayside accidents raise their tuckers too often," that although they "may continue pure, yet we cannot help remembering the assaults which have lifted their petticoats" (Rawson, 292). Taine blames Fielding for being too coarse, for including everything in his novels except refinement. Yet the very same incidents adduced by Taine to prove Fielding's indelicacy are those advanced by Aldous Huxley in praise of Fielding for telling "the whole truth"; Sophia's embarrassing fall at the inn door, which exposes her charms to the sniggering yokels, for instance, certifies Fielding's claim to be a truth teller rather than a censor of life in the interests of an artificial dignity.[5] What Taine deplores, Huxley applauds, in a head-on collision of irreconcilable views. This, as we shall find, is a paradigm case; almost every episode, every passage, in *Tom Jones* is hospitable to censure or celebration, as the critics queue up to refute each other, bringing a yea to counter each nay. Byron's portrait of the social revolutionary, bent on exposing the great (Rawson, 244), almost inevitably leads to Leslie Stephen's view of the antirevolutionary Whig (Rawson, 304); Orbilius's "filthy author" (Rawson, 110–113) becomes in the twentieth century, according to James A. Work, the Christian censor (*Lit. Crit.*, 233–34).

The arguments provoked by the book have raged over three separate yet related questions: Is it moral or immoral? Is it reprehensibly "low" or laudably realistic? Is it technically inept or a masterpiece of artistic construction? Occasionally, as in the onslaughts of Richardson and Johnson, the book is arraigned as exhibiting all these faults simultaneously; occasionally, as in Coleridge's ovation, the book is exalted for displaying the full set of virtues. To simplify this survey, each individual indictment, together with the answering defense, will be considered separately.

From the outset *Tom Jones* was denounced as immoral, as a book with a tendency to deprave and corrupt. Richardson identifies this as Fielding's second motive (the first was to make money): "to whiten a vicious character, and to make morality bend to his practices." Richardson lists its objectionable elements: the hero is illegitimate; the heroine goes traipsing after the scapegrace, a fugitive from her father's house; she is a foolish, insipid female, illustrating Fielding's inability to depict a delicate woman because he had never been used to such company (Rawson, 107–108). "In an age so dissolute as the present what can be said for the morality (for the morality shall I say?) propagated in *Tom Jones?*" (Rawson, 108). The indignant incredulity of the parenthesis is its own answer, and Richardson hammers in the last nail by laying everything at the door of the author's own bad life: "Do men expect grapes of thorns or figs of thistles?" The summary is magisterially decisive: "A dissolute book. Its run is over, even with us" (Rawson, 116).

Johnson concurs, finding Richardson as superior to Fielding in virtue as in talent. He tongue-lashes Hannah More for frivolously letting slip that she had read *Tom Jones:* "I am shocked to hear you quote from so vicious a book. I am sorry to hear you have read it; a confession which no modest lady should ever make. I scarcely know a more corrupt work" (Rawson, 181). It is the tone, almost the words, of Parson Manders scolding the freethinking Mrs. Alving in the first act of *Ghosts:* outraged morality is the more livid when the culprit is female. In 1749 Orbilius weighed in with a hundred-page review of the "fetid foundling" and its "filthy author," a view, more moderately expressed, that was to find its champions for almost a century. (When, in a later phase, Ford Madox Ford attacked *Tom Jones* as immoral, he was using the word in the Wildean sense to lambaste bad art). From Lady Mary Wortley Montagu onward, a series of critics—Oliver Goldsmith, Cobbett, Thackeray—pointed to the morally harmful consequences of reading *Tom Jones,* especially the threat to the young. It was a menace to public morals; an offensive example of pernicious romance, deluding young men into believing that a life of dissipation and folly will somehow end in riches and matrimony; boys and virgins must read it with caution (Rawson, 132, 155–56, 400, 263). Fielding, it is charged by Hester Chapone, "takes his notions of human nature from the most depraved and corrupted part of it, and seems to think no character natural, but such as are a disgrace to the human species" (Rawson, 126). This is a remarkable accusation, if true, because this is precisely why Tom attacks the Man of the Hill. Thackeray echoes Richardson's biographical explication: "the great humourist's moral sense was blunted by his life . . . he is himself the hero of his books: he is wild Tom Jones, he is wild Captain Booth" (Rawson, 278, 274). Ruskin seconds Orbilius in his disgust at Tobias Smollett and Fielding, "licking their chops over nastiness, like hungry dogs over ordure" (Rawson, 262).

Yet voices, admittedly less numerous, less authoritative, had from the beginning defended *Tom Jones*. Arthur Murphy, Fielding's first biographer, despite originating the myth of the dissipated rake—W. E. Henley was to explode this simply by reminding us that the thousands of hours that went into the creation of *Tom Jones* reveal no bibulous wastrel but a great and serious artist (Rawson, 324)—argued that the book was a styptic to the sensual imagination, preventing rather than promoting corruption: "*Tom Jones* will at all times be a fine lesson to young men of good tendencies to virtue, who yet suffer the impetuosity of their passions to hurry them away" (Rawson, 167).

By the new century change was imminent. Walter Scott declared that only those already inclined to corruption would be corrupted by *Tom Jones* (Rawson, 235). Coleridge challenges Johnson by attacking Richardson as a moralist and denouncing *Clarissa* as poisonous to the mind (Rawson, 204). Fielding's laughter is hailed as the healthy antidote to a hyperactive libido; sex as comic romp is the classic defense against Richardson's obsession with the pornographic melodrama of claustrophobic bedrooms. If anyone threatens youthful innocence, it is the prurient, lingering, voyeuristic Richardson, not his healthily animalistic rival. Thackeray even sighs enviously for the sexual openness now denied to the Victorian novelist (Rawson, 263–64). There are no dark places in Fielding's writing; what some modern critics condescendingly or complainingly remark is what Coleridge points to as his highest merit. Byron chuckles over the fact that *Clarissa* is now used to wrap cheese while Fielding, the prose Homer of human nature, flourishes (Rawson, 237). Increasingly, *Tom Jones* will be celebrated as a major weapon in the war against shams—Walter Raleigh declared it "the epic of youth . . . no truer, saner book has ever been written" (*Lit. Crit.*, 217–18)—and Fielding acclaimed as the heir of Aristophanes and Molière.

Clearly, the attacks on *Tom Jones* were not simply inspired by its content—Richardson's work contains seductions and rapes aplenty— but by Fielding's attitude to it. That he stood for a new approach to fiction, a new attitude to life, was recognized from the outset. Francis Coventry praised "the new species of writing lately introduc'd by Mr. Fielding" for showing that pure nature could be as entertaining as fantastic romance. *Tom Jones* was "a lively representative of real life. For chrystal palaces and winged horses, we find homely cots and ambling nags; and instead of impossibility, what we experience every day" (*Lit. Crit.*, 206–207). Fielding's problem, to be confronted in a much intensified form by Flaubert and Joyce, is how to make everyday experience interesting.

In attempting to balance the claims of literary tradition and contemporary reality, of perfected art and moral actuality, Fielding did not please everyone. *Tom Jones* extends the franchise of fictional representation to hitherto underprivileged classes, despised occupations, neglected social settings, and for some this is its great achievement: "Where is the novel in existence which has reached so many corners of society?" asks George Barnett Smith (*Lit. Crit.*, 215). But for Richardson the price of this extension was too high, and he expresses a disgust at the very substance of Fielding's achievement: "Who can care for any of his people?" (Rawson, 131). Dr. Johnson similarly rejects the idea of realism as self-justifying; when Boswell praised Fielding for drawing "very natural pictures of human life," Johnson countered, "it is of very low life."[6] He even accuses Fielding of using realism as a device for confusing the reader's moral responses by perplexingly mingling good with bad qualities in the same character, and, remarkably, denies the relevance of realism altogether: "It is therefore not a sufficient vindication of a character, that it is drawn as it appears, for many characters ought never to be drawn" (Rawson, 115–16). Fielding's achievement becomes a demerit; he is a low writer trading in low material. As Hazlitt remarks in reprimanding Fielding's prim censurers, it is not the scenes in the alehouse but the alehouse itself that offends.[7]

What makes the lapse the more unpardonable is its recreant element, because the aristocratically connected Fielding ought to have known better. "Had your brother . . . been born in a stable, or been a runner at a sponging-house, we should have thought him a genius, and wished he had had the advantages of a liberal education, and of being admitted into good company"—so wrote Richardson to Sarah Fielding on 23 February 1752 (Rawson, 131). But what is one to do with someone who deliberately sins against the light, who intentionally writes books in which "the women are drabs, and the men scoundrels"? Simply mourn the squandering of the precious talent, the betrayal of the privileged birthright. "It has grieved me to see so much power as you have possessed, employed to so little purpose as you have employed it" (Rawson, 133). Neither Richardson nor Johnson can forgive the class traitor whose demagoguery Colley Cibber had already denounced: "to draw the mob after him he must rake the channel and pelt their superiors" (Rawson, 49).

Fielding's defenders, such as Elizabeth Carter and Arthur Murphy, responded by praising as realism what his detractors condemned as low. *Tom Jones* is "the most natural representation of what passes in the world"; its characters "look . . . act . . . speak to our imagination just as they appear to us in the world" (Rawson, 105, 167). Clara Reeve defines the achievement: "he certainly painted human nature as it is rather than as it ought to be" (Rawson, 186); and Hazlitt agrees: "It smacked of the world I lived in, and in which I was to live" (Rawson, 188). Robert Burns takes the offensive on Fielding's behalf, condemning Richardson's characters as unreal (Rawson, 189). Walter Scott contemplates the squandered, irregular life that Richardson deplores, and finds there the key to Fielding's greatness, social misfortune transformed to a novelist's *felix culpa*—for only in this way had he become acquainted with all classes in society, and so led to ground his art on "truth and human nature itself" (*Lit. Crit.*, 211). As the nineteenth century unfolded, and ideas of hierarchy and decorum in art and society alike began to fade, complaints about Fielding's "lowness" became sparser. Why blame the mirror for the reality it reflects? Taine applauds Fielding for upholding the mortifying standard of reality, for continuing Molière's mission of showing men and women with their masks off, for "lifting a corner of the cloak" (*Lit. Crit.*, 213–14). That the Squares of this world are resentful simply confirms the salutariness of the exposure. In the new, more democratic, more egalitarian age, there was no more mileage left in denouncing Fielding as low.

Relief in this quarter, however, simply cleared the way for the most serious, damaging accusation of all: the attack upon *Tom Jones* as an artistically incompetent work. Here, too, there is outright disagreement from the start, with the detractors having the better of the early exchanges. Richardson told Sarah Fielding that *Tom Jones* reveals "the knowledge of the outside of a clockwork machine" rather than "of all the finer springs of movement of the inside" (Rawson, 155), and the same depreciatory image is employed by Dr. Johnson to demote Fielding's art to a mere matter of surface fidelity (Rawson, 173–74). Admirers like Sir Walter Scott might praise "the felicitous contrivances, and happy extrication of the story, where every incident tells upon, and advances the catastrophe" (Rawson, 233), but opponents from Johnson to Kermode dismissively retort, "clockwork" (*Lit. Crit.*, 237–38). The "artful management," the "perfection of fable," detected by Murphy (Rawson, 166), do not impress those like Leavis who sabotage the whole idea of perfect construction by objecting that the book has no serious subject matter, no important human concerns, to construct.[8] Dr. Johnson had likewise awarded the palm to Richardson by saying that he creates characters of nature, lastingly important, while Fielding merely assembles meccano characters of manners, transiently trivial (Rawson, 173).

It is pointless to tell Ford that no novel in the language has been so artfully conducted or that its author is one of the most minutely careful artists who ever lived; he simply retorts that "the introductory chapters make me sick" and that "there are few books that I more cordially dislike than *Tom Jones*." It is "one of the most immoral books ever written"—in style, not content—"a dreadful example of how not to do things" (Rawson, 346–47, 353). What disgusts him most of all is what other critics have found most admirable in the book: the intrusive, controlling narrator; the essays, digressions, interpolations, which, far from being a hindrance, create a bond between author and reader, unifying the novel, highlighting its philosophical theme; the artistic conduct of a complicated plot, which evoked Coleridge's famous tribute—all this is detestable to Ford. The spectacle of Fielding fussing over his narrative as a hen over her chicks, of the misguided artist archly pirouetting and winking across his pages, is, for Ford, insupportable.

Yet Gide calls *Tom Jones* a masterpiece and consulted it assiduously during the writing of his own masterpiece, *The Counterfeiters* (Rawson, 352). Thackeray's view of *Tom Jones*—"as a work of construction, quite a wonder" (Rawson, 277)—has also had its defenders from the beginning. Fielding has been praised as the most important contributor to the development of the English novel, as the writer under whom the genre reached maturity as an art form. Scott hails him as England's first great novelist, and salutes the essays and digressions as "an experiment in British literature" (Rawson, 230, 237). Byron is equally enthusiastic; for him, Fielding is not, as Lord Monboddo would have it, just a primitive, mixing essay with novel because he knows no better (Rawson, 177); rather he is what today might be called an antinovelist, playing games with an already established art of realistic narrative, "sporting with his subject—its master, not its slave" (Rawson, 238). This sense of aristocratic mastery would naturally appeal to Byron against Richardson's dutifully bourgeois subservience to the demands of realism.

Today, Fielding's supporters insist that its alleged faults are so only on the supposition that *Tom Jones* should have been another kind of novel. Martin C. Battestin, for instance, argues that *Joseph Andrews* was written not in negation of *Pamela* but in affirmation of a fresh and antithetical theory of the art of the novel (*Lit. Crit.*, 251), and that this holds a fortiori for *Tom Jones*, which is a critique of Richardson not only in content but in style, not merely by what it *says* but by what it *is*. Ford's blunder is a failure to see that the offending narrator is really a rich and provocative chorus whose wisdom, learning, and benevolence permeate the world of the book.[9] Moreover, the book is a thoroughly Augustan novel that presents a solid, assured world, a stable social order in which every individual finds his proper place, and offers a clear-cut, commonsense Christianity as a guide for action. Naturally, order is the keynote of the narrative as well, with the narrator, a secular analogue of Providence, in control of a complex yet finally unified structure.[10] In his capacity as Creator, Fielding contains in his mind the totality of his creation—the whole notion of plot rests on the presupposition that a unique design exists which is true though not yet apparent. Indeed, so established has this reading become that it has provoked a reaction. For some critics—Ronald Paulson, for example—the "Christianizing" of Fielding has gone too far; what was originally an important corrective has become a diversion from his real achievement, which is, *not* the medicine of Christian morality, but the disease for which it is prescribed (*Lit. Crit.*, 255).

Richardson and Fielding were fated to be foes from the outset, and even in death they pursue their antagonisms in circumstances they could never have foreseen. They continue to exhibit the ability to divide opinion that they possessed from the first. They have been conscripted, for example, as combatants in our contemporary debate over feminism: Katharine M. Rogers depicts Richardson as a writer sympathetic to women who shows them as autonomous beings rather than as mere appendages to fathers, husbands, brothers, or lovers, while she sees Fielding's work as conditioned by the antifeminist prejudices of his time (*Lit. Crit.*, 263–65).

Both writers reacted against Restoration licentiousness by condemning the sexual exploitation of women, their reduction to sex objects; Fielding denounces those who regard women as meat or prey. Both opposed the libertine view that men lose by marriage and attacked the double standard of sexual morality, though Fielding is more vulnerable on this point. Both accepted, on the whole, the hierarchical structure of the eighteenth-century family, which required women to obey parents and husbands. But Richardson's is a more radical response to the new sensibility about women that probes traditional assumptions about male-female relationships, especially in his revolutionary suggestion of marriage as a partnership. Fielding, despite his humane disposition, is alleged to have accepted the male chauvinism of his culture and to have incorporated the new sensibility into the old system of male dominance and conventional relationships. His good women seem dependent on masculine approval and love, existing only to serve the men they live with. Richardson invites women to converse with men, to discuss any topic as equals. Fielding, by contrast, appears to single out as a particular excellence Sophia's self-effacing refusal to express an opinion, even when pressed to do so by Allworthy, Thwackum, and Square. Despite his urging, Allworthy is delighted at this refusal, and Fielding presumably agrees (784). Women who too readily express opinions tend to be immodest and dictatorial (Mrs. Western is a flagrant culprit), deficient in that awe of the masculine mind which Fielding is said to have considered appropriate. Other readers may think that awe is scarcely the response solicited by Fielding to the lucubrations of Thwackum and Square, or that Squire Western is hardly offered as a proof of the superiority of the masculine mind.

Whatever our view of this or of any other particular dispute, the essential truth remains: here are living texts, not antiquarian records, retaining the power to divide us as vehemently today as they have divided readers since their first appearance. Of *Tom Jones* in particular we may confidently give the lie to Richardson's dogmatically hostile diktat: its run is *not* over.

A Reading

4

Fighting the Pharisees

Toward the close of the novel the newly enlightened Allworthy, swinging between self-reproach for having been so long blind to Tom's goodness, and censure of Tom for the sustained imprudence that mitigates his myopia, breaks off to pay his auditor the supreme Fielding compliment: "hypocrisy (good Heaven how have I been imposed on by it in others!) was never among your faults" (853). For this much else can be forgiven. It is better to be a sinner than a hypocrite. There is always hope where there is no hypocrisy; only the hypocrite, the Pharisee, stands obdurately outside the pull of salvation. Hypocrisy, says Hazlitt, is the only vice that cannot be forgiven, because even the repentance of a hypocrite is hypocritical.[1] Fielding, indeed, provides a perfect exemplum in his final depiction of the groveling Blifil, despicable and degraded, sorry not for his sins but for their detection. Be what you will, a thief like Black George, a coward like Partridge, a highwayman like Anderson, a kept man like Jones, and you still have a chance of rescue; but the Pharisee is damned.

Yet scholars tell us that the historical Pharisees may have been maligned and misreported.[2] They were, after all, the one element of traditional Judaism to survive the destruction of Jerusalem and the dispersal of its people. As such they inevitably attracted the hostility of the early Christians, who rightly identified them as their most dangerous religious competitors. St. Paul told King Agrippa that he had been brought up as a Pharisee, within the strictest sect in Israel (Acts 26:5). Perhaps, paradoxically, it was their very virtues that provoked their enemies to a defamation so successful that the name itself has become a synonym for corruption. It is highly possible that Pharisaism has been made out to be worse than it really was.

The truth of this must be left to the scholars to determine; for the purpose of the argument here, Pharisaism will be understood in the traditional, possibly slanderous, sense of the word. Yet even here, on the evidence of the Gospels themselves, it soon becomes clear that Pharisaism sustains two very different, perhaps even contradictory, interpretations, initially distinguishable as deception and self-deception. The first, most obvious definition of Pharisee is hypocrite, fraud, pious dissembler, someone whose virtue is a pose, an act, a performance; who deceives others, but knows himself. Tartuffe at once comes to mind, or Square, posing as the Stoic wise man who has overcome the body, chastising Tom for his shameful surrender to sexual passion, before being himself found crouched humiliatingly with the *other* female utensils beside Molly's bed. Both John the Baptist and Jesus denounce the Pharisees along these lines. The Baptist calls them "snakes" and warns them to prove by their actions (the only acceptable proof) that they have turned from sin: "every tree that does not bear good fruit will be cut down and thrown into the fire." Words alone, faith without works, are futile; the test is action: "He will reward each one according to his deeds" (Matt. 3:7–10). The branch that does not bear fruit is simply firewood. Fielding, as we shall see, is a fervent advocate of the Baptist's ethos; in *Joseph Andrews* he specifically invites the reader to join him in condemning the pernicious doctrine of faith without works as the bane of true Christianity.[3]

Jesus, if anything, surpasses the Baptist in virulence. The Pharisees are blind guides, rapacious engrossers of widows' houses, serpents, broods of vipers, persecutors of the prophets, and enemies of the just; above all, they are barren ritualists, sterile legalists, obsessively preoccupied with appearances and forms while flouting in their hearts the basic religious and moral decencies: "Woe to you, Scribes and Pharisees! because you are like whited sepulchres, which out-wardly appear to men beautiful, but within you are full of dead men's bones and of all uncleanness. So you also outwardly appear just to men, but within you are full of hypocrisy and iniquity" (Matt. 23:27–28). Against no other sin does Jesus fulminate so fiercely; the invective is pitiless, the rage almost ungovernable, as he strips bare the impu-dicity of this bogus virtue.

Yet there is another and different type of Pharisee, neither hypo-critical rogue nor fraudulent trickster. The Pharisee presented by Jesus in his parable is not some Palestinian precursor of Tartuffe, but a good man, sincere and devout, speaking the simple truth. He *had* done all he said—prayed, fasted, paid tithes, given alms; he was *not* lying when he thanked God that he was not greedy, dishonest, adulterous, like other men. True, he despised the publican at the back of the temple, but what good man would not? Publican, tax collector—such words were mere synonyms for rogue and swindler, people with whom it was morally impossible to share the same table. To associate with such was in itself a contamination, about as sensible as becoming the crony of lepers or sharing a needle with heroin addicts. For Jesus even to sug-gest that the tax swindler found more favor with God than the devout Pharisee was outrageous—but, then, so too was his parable of the prodigal son. In having the abandoned, disreputable wretch come off better with his father than the upright son who stayed at home, Jesus must have seemed to many of the righteous in Israel to be undermining the very foundations of morality and justice.

If Jesus lashed the first kind of Pharisee for deceit, this second kind was equally scandalized by what they could only interpret as his own disgraceful laxity. The Pharisee believes above all in the law as a system of ritualized external performances; believes that he has been elected by God to be the vigilant custodian and scrupulous servant of the law; and believes that everyone who deviates from the law, how-ever minutely, should be punished in accordance with God's com-mand. Simon the Pharisee was genuinely shocked when Jesus allowed the prostitute to anoint his feet with the precious ointment; surely a true prophet would have recognized the identity of the ministrant, and surely a good man would have driven her away in loathing? Simon, a good man himself, would certainly have done so. This second kind of Pharisee was distinguished by true zeal for the law, for cultic purity and ritual exactitude, for ostentatious devotion, and for works of supererogation as evoking, almost compelling, God's favor.

Jesus, by contrast, displays an astonishing freedom toward the law, which the Pharisee could only regard as criminal negligence. Not for him the pious legalism, the stern Sabbatarianism, of the strict moralist. However much he revered the law, he never hesitated to act against it when he thought fit, whether it meant healing on the Sabbath or preventing the stoning of the adulteress. Although not abolishing the law, he did not shrink from placing himself (and mankind) above it. No wonder the Pharisees were outraged by his friendship with gluttons, drinkers, loose livers, law breakers; this, reinforced by such parables as the prodigal son and the Pharisee and the publican, must have seemed morally subversive, destructive and offensive, to many decent, godfearing Israelites. Jesus as moral teacher is altogether too slack, too lackadaisical, for the hard-line Pharisee mentality.

Yet, paradoxically, Jesus, the forgiver of sinners, the bender of rules, coming between the hard-liners and their righteous prey, the adulteress, is also, in another sense, much harsher, more condemnatory, than his adversaries. Legalism is, after all, intended as a friendly, a consoling, service to humanity, relieving man's conscience, providing security. If you avoid certain actions, if you scrupulously perform others, then you can rest easy in the assurance of God's favor; so taught the Pharisees (so they teach still), freeing man from the anguish of his dubious salvation. Jesus, making light of the purity regulations, of the need for clean hands, insisted instead that only purity of heart counted with God. The consequence is that he is at once more demanding and more lenient than his opponents. The Pharisees condemned violence against others as sinful; Jesus points to the anger that fuels violence as the root offense. The Pharisees warned men against the act of adultery; Jesus tells us to avoid the very thought, since he who dreams of adultery has already committed it. Sin is not, as the Pharisees taught, an act, something done, external; it is a wish, something desired, internal. Hence Jesus' rage against the self-righteous sinner, hence the striking metaphor of the beautifully whitened tombs that house dead men's bones. Such "piety" simply masks a craving for public acclaim; it ministers to vanity, to a theatricality that has already had its reward.

Salvation is, accordingly, a much more problematic and nerve-racking matter than that computed by the Pharisees, those actuaries of virtue. Even the "good" Pharisee, visiting God to discuss his spiritual balance sheet much as he might visit the bank manager about his financial one, has got things hopelessly confused. Against the Pharisees, fixated on moral accountancy, forever balancing merit against sin, Jesus insisted that there was no question of merit at all. Salvation is not the reward of merit but the largesse of grace; it has nothing to do with man's deserving, but is simply God's gift, free, unconditional, like the good heart that Tom Jones was born with. It defies and affronts human calculation, as the parable of the laborers in the vineyard, with its scandal of equal pay for all, so disconcertingly displays. We are not to compute what God owes us, a vulgar error to which, as Jesus points out, good people are especially prone. The sinner is too busy asking for mercy to demand his deserts. It's the person conscious of his own worth, in particular of his superiority to the scapegrace at the rear of the temple, who reminds God of the fine fellow he is; it's the man who has toiled all day in the vineyard who is indignant when he learns that some Johnny-come-lately is to receive the same wages as himself.

However humanly understandable such resentment may be, it is, Jesus insists, totally inappropriate when applied to the relationship between God and man. Yet it seems rooted in human nature—how difficult it is not to be continually comparing ourselves with others. Nevertheless, Christ is remorseless to those who do compare themselves with others, invariably to their own advantage. For it is not the tax collectors who find it hard to repent; it is the devout, convinced as they already are of their own justification. Anyone without self-criticism takes himself too seriously, while simultaneously taking God and his fellowmen too lightly. It was, after all, the good people who engineered the Crucifixion, and who thought they were thereby serving God by punishing the blasphemer. If the good people renege on their duty of punishing sinners, the consequences for the public good will be disastrous: so ran, so still runs, the argument.

Every other consideration aside, this last point should alert us to the significance of all this for an understanding of *Tom Jones*. Almost from the opening page the novel becomes the forum for a debate as to how we should deal with sinners and try to reform sin. Allworthy is continually reprehended for what Thwackum, as leading Pharisee, regards as his criminal lenity in handling sin; Thwackum, by contrast, trusts to the whip as the infallible recipe for promoting virtue. But the most cursory reader of Fielding's novel soon discovers that it goes much deeper than a seminar on effective penology, on rehabilitation and retribution; in *Tom Jones* Fielding set out to scrutinize, to appraise and evaluate, the various forms and manifestations of Pharisaism, to provide a complete taxonomy of the malady, from the most impudent hypocrisy to the most deep-seated self-righteousness. Unless we remind ourselves that Fielding is to the Pharisees what Samson was to the Philistines—their fated foe and destined destroyer—we shall inevitably go astray, baffled by the apparent contradictions in the man and his work. The next chapter will examine how the struggle against Pharisaism conditioned the very style and form of the novel, how the need to expose the Pharisee—not merely the Pharisee as character *within* the text, but the Pharisee as potential reader *of* the text— shaped the kind of fiction that the pioneering author chose to create. For the moment it will suffice to point to the magisterial element in Fielding's art. *Tom Jones* has been described as an exercise in the pursuit of true judgment;[4] it seeks to educate, to train its reader to be a good judge—which, by definition, means to avoid being a Pharisee. The Pharisee is the worst of judges, at once too severe and too indulgent, too possessed by arrogance in his dealings with others, too lacking in spiritual modesty, in moral imagination, when interrogating himself.

To be a good judge of the text, one must see from the outset how provocatively and aggressively it challenges Pharisaism. Those who miss this are at risk of falling into various errors concerning Fielding and his book. The less harmful blunder is the myth of the genial Fielding, a jolly fellow, always ready, like his hero Tom, for another glass and another woman, reckless and unrefined, but full of a vulgar vitality, so that his book, though not really important, is a jolly good read and a triumph of the Augustan picaresque. Far more damaging than this good-natured, if trivializing, estimate is the more hostile view of Fielding as a bad man, corrupt and corrupting, a cynical debunker of any real goodness, whose vicious book—Dr. Johnson knew no more corrupt work (Rawson, 181)—is the appropriate poisonous fruit of his own contaminated self. To recognize Fielding as the foe of the Pharisees is to avoid each of these critical pitfalls.

Fielding enters the arena as a comedian, but I shall postpone until the final chapter a consideration of his comedy, aside from pointing out that he is a comedian not because he is careless but because he is Christian—his comedy stems from faith much more than from experience: *credo quia impossibile est.* He enters the fray as adversary of the Pharisees on two main counts: he proposes, not, as Dr. Johnson would have it, a cancellation of morality, but a revaluation of values, a new league table, as it were, of sins, in direct subversion of the priorities of Pharisaism; and he recommends a "new" way (really as old as the Gospels, but continually ignored) of dealing with transgressors—namely, recourse to punishment only as a last, desperate, unavoidable resort, rather than as the panacea preached so avidly by the Pharisees. Denouncing those who instinctively reach for the whip, who love to lash, he links together the most disparate types—self-righteous moralists, hidebound Calvinists, snarling, malicious critics—but all united as condemners of men (302, 468, 509). Fielding follows Jesus in condemning the condemners. Conversely, he brings pardon to sinners, leaning over backwards to palliate any fault, to excuse any offender, thief, highwayman, fornicator, just as long as he is not also a hypocrite.

This antipathy to the hypocrite is not simply the thoughtless, instinctively defensive reaction of the jolly dog, *l'homme moyen sensuel,* toward the censorious sneak who would spoil his fun. It is a pondered condemnation, grounded in the most strenuous moral objections to hypocrisy as the sin against the Holy Spirit, the unforgivable sin that bars the route to heaven, the defect that drew from Jesus his fiercest invective. Ideally, a man should exhibit his true self to the world, not only *being* but *acting* himself, matching word to deed, motive to action, performance to promise, existence to essence, in perfect concordance. Outside and inside should mesh in exact congruence. Such perfect symmetry will, admittedly, be achieved only at the Last Judgment, when reputation and reality finally meet in permanent, indissoluble unity; on earth there will always be a discrepancy, an unavoidable disproportion, between truth and seeming. The choice is between presenting to the world the false face of the Pharisee, or, as Fielding recommends, wearing a face that is not more but less comely than the real one. What good is it, morally speaking, to have the face of an archbishop and the heart of a miller? Better, declares Fielding, to seem worse than to seem better than you are, better—the question of worldly success apart—for a man to misrepresent himself downwards, to be his own traducer, the concealer of his true worth, than to pose as a better man than he truly is or to claim virtues not his own. Better for Tom Jones to seem a drunken and libidinous wastrel than for Blifil to seem the impassioned liberator of caged birds.

When we press Fielding to justify this preference, we touch the core of his Christian comedy. In his optimistic secularization of Christian eschatology, his earthly rendition of the Last Judgment, the *parousia*, all things will be revealed in time, with an inevitable reappraisal and revision of reputations. In that there must be such a revision, let it be upwards. When the day of disclosure comes, woe to the man who has been valued above his deserts, whose reward has exceeded his merit; such a man, like a moral bankrupt, has been living beyond his means; when, at Judgment Day, the checks inevitably bounce, he will be the more discomfited. Conversely, the man who has been devalued or misprized will be justified and raised to his proper level.

Fielding could have cited the highest scriptural authority for his preference in Christ's advice to those about to attend a feast. Those who presumptuously claim the first place at table run the risk of humiliation when the lord of the feast decides his own seating arrangements. The wise guest will guard against the shame of being publicly ordered to a lower place; only the spiritually modest will hear the gratifyingly welcome words: "Friend, go up higher! Then thou wilt be honored in the presence of all who are at table with thee. For everyone who exalts himself shall be humbled, and he who humbles himself shall be exalted" (Luke 14:7). No Pharisee will ever be the recipient of these words; having already arrogated to himself the place of honor at the Lord's table, he will suffer either dismissal to a lower station or banishment from the feast altogether.

It is in this sense that Fielding's otherwise misleading opening metaphor of the novel as feast and the novelist as restaurateur is so strikingly pertinent. Fielding's novel is not an inn where we can sit where we choose and eat what we will; if we do behave in this unmannerly fashion, we will, as we shall see, be quickly ordered to take our unwelcome custom elsewhere (51). I shall be considering later the series of metaphors by which Fielding attempts to define his relationship to the reader. For the present it is enough to say that if the novel is a feast, it is so in the sense of the passage just quoted from the Gospel of St. Luke—a feast in which the guests, characters and readers alike, will be judged and allocated. Blifil, the chief Pharisee, lacking the proper garment, will be bound hand and foot and cast into exterior darkness (scarcely the kind of treatment to be encountered in the average hotel), while Tom, unjustly banished from Paradise Hall, at least partly as a consequence of his own self-depreciation, will be restored to his true position as Allworthy's heir.

Fielding's fondness for parable has often been remarked, usually in terms of a predilection for the illuminating cameo, the striking vignette, the revealing incident, within the text, that provides the clue to the essential moral meaning. What has not been adequately recognized is that *Tom Jones,* considered as a total structure, is a complex and elaborate extension of one of the simplest yet most profound of the parables, that of the two sons. Beneath the ample flesh of the panoramic display of eighteenth-century English society is the bare skeleton of the parable, providing the armature of the work. When the father ordered his first son to go and work in the vineyard, the boy refused; but, afterwards, countermanding his own words, he obeyed the command and performed the work. By contrast, the second son instantly promised to obey, but did nothing. For each, word and deed clash, and appearances are misleading: the good son seems disobedient and ungrateful, the bad son a model of filial rectitude. No one can miss the parable's meaning. Certainly, the Pharisees, who had been harrying Jesus and to whom the parable was addressed, did not. When Jesus asked them which of the two sons had done his father's will, they, giving the only possible answer, walked straight into the trap set for them: "Amen I say to you, the publicans and harlots are entering the kingdom of God before you" (Matt. 21:28–32).

Just as unmistakable as the parable's meaning is its pertinence to the central concern of Fielding's novel. Once again we have the two sons (technically Bridget's, but, in terms of the legacy of golden girl and golden mountain, the possession of Sophia and Paradise Hall, they are Allworthy's boys, only one of whom can be finally fortunate); the novel's resolution shows the long-deluded Allworthy that the apparent rapscallion is the true son who has really done the father's will, while the dutiful yes-man, so punctiliously pious, is really a rogue and a hypocrite. The reader, if not Allworthy, should have no difficulty in making these identifications from the start. When we hear that young Master Blifil possessed "a zeal surprising in one so young," alarm bells should start to ring; is not this, above all else, the spoor of the Pharisee, made all the more unmistakable by the youth of the offender? (135). When, much earlier, his uncle, the doctor, is described as having "a great appearance of religion," we intuit instantly that this is bogus, a front for a very different reality (75). Distrust appearances: things are not what they seem; God's judgment is not man's; the best of men are blunderers (Allworthy is not all-seeing), while the worst are cheats. Fielding is doing little more than give body to the moral teachings of Jesus, applying the Gospel's ethical insights in his new fiction. Gide accused Fielding of being unable to conceive a saint, which is simply a pejorative way of saying that he distrusted a too visibly strenuous

striving after virtue—as did Jesus when he warned those doing good
not to let the left hand know what the right was up to.

Tom, in contrast to his mealymouthed rival, is thoughtless, giddy,
with little sobriety of manner, wild and impulsive—which is promis-
ing, because it means he is his natural self rather than an unnatural
impostor, a tearaway but not a prig. How can we fail to see in this
description of the two boys—the elder born to be hanged, the other a
model youth—a replication of the parable's antithesis: the first defying
the father, the other all sweet obedience? But, lest we do, Fielding
supplies throughout the text a succession of incidents and situations
that drive home the Gospel provenance of his fiction. Tom's friendship
with Black George exposes him to the same charge brought by the
Pharisees against Jesus for his unsavory associations with the dregs of
Jerusalem: would a good man consort with publicans and harlots?
Thwackum and Square likewise attempt to blacken the boy in Allworthy's estimate by pointing to the company he keeps. Tom is by no
means a messiah (though by the later stages of the novel this identifi-
cation will cease to be so farfetched or outrageous), but we do find
him suffering for the sins of others and taking all the blame for sin
upon himself. The parallel with Jesus extends to his enemies' slander.
The Pharisees accused Jesus of casting out demons with the help of
demons; thus his seeming good was really evil. Square follows suit
when he persuades Allworthy that the apparent goodness of Tom is
really corruption, that he relieved the Seagrim family as a path to Molly's bed, helping the parents in order to debauch the daughter. Of
course, Tom is *not* Jesus—but just as surely his enemies *are* the Pharisees, the enemies of Jesus.

The clinching proof of this is supplied when that even more ut-
terly improbable *alter Christus*, Squire Western, uses the very words
of Jesus to the Pharisees in condemnation of Tom's detractors. It occurs as the culmination of a series of visits by the foremost Pharisees
to the bedside of Tom, who lies recuperating from the broken arm he
suffered when rescuing Sophia (203–204). Thwackum, Square, Blifil,
each arrives in turn, ostensibly to comfort the sufferer, but really to
tell him what a bad lot he is and how deserved or, in Square's case,

how trivially insignificant is his anguish. Thwackum assures Tom that the broken arm is a sign from heaven, a judgment upon the sinner— not, of course, to encourage Tom to repent, since that is impossible, but to give him a foretaste of the pangs of hell, his inevitable desti- nation. An angry God, alert to the affair with Molly, has broken Tom's arm, in much the same way, if we are to accept certain contemporary views, that he has sent AIDS today as a visitation on sinful man. Square, for his part, tells the sufferer that pain is contemptible, a trifle that the Stoic wise man easily ignores, before accidentally biting his own tongue and giving way to an outburst of grief and anger. Blifil visits seldom and never alone, because isolated proximity to a sinner (the AIDS analogy again) can be a risky business.

Western is the last of the visitors—rowdy, drunken, trying to force beer down the patient's throat, riotously disturbing his much-needed rest, but, redeeming all else, good-natured and meaning well (204– 205). The point is vital to an understanding of Fielding's ethic. The road to *heaven* is paved with good intentions. An ostensibly virtuous act (the freeing of a bird, telling the truth) when motivated by malice is an abomination; conversely, a reckless or even technically sinful act (Tom's lie to save Black George from punishment) may be forgiven or even commended, provided the motive is good. Fielding anticipates the insight of T. S. Eliot's saintly martyr: the greatest treason is to do the right deed for the wrong reason.[5] Just as clearly he also anticipates Graham Greene's insight concerning his saintly sinners: that to damn oneself for the good of others, like Scobie or the whiskey priest, may be the highest virtue of all. The smug hypocrites who tiptoe demurely and maliciously toward Tom's sickbed are in far worse moral case than the rowdy, well-meaning drunkard.

Admittedly, Western's defense of Tom against the hypocrites has its selfish side; Tom broke his arm protecting Western's daughter, so the squire is most unlikely to take the same churlishly uncharitable view of the injury as Thwackum. Nevertheless, his stinging rebuke to Tom's vilifier is astonishing as we hear the violent, uncontrollable drunkard unwittingly echoing the words of Christ to the Pharisees: "I have had a battle for thee below stairs with thick parson

Thwackum.—He hath been a telling Allworthy, before my face, that the broken bone was a judgement upon thee. D - - n it, says I, how can that be? Did not he come by it in defence of a young woman? A judgement indeed! Pox, if he never doth anything worse, he will go to heaven sooner than all the parsons in the country" (205–206). Expletives and imprecations apart, we are listening to the judgment of Jesus: "the publicans and harlots are entering the kingdom of God before you." Not those who talk, serving God with their tongues only, however mellifluous, but those who do their father's will, however low their social reputation: these are the true heirs of the kingdom. But Thwackum was doubtless as affronted to hear Tom preferred above him as were the righteous in Israel to hear of the new, shockingly subversive order of entry into the kingdom.

The sickbed visits reveal, in addition, the classic Pharisee explanation of human suffering. Thwackum's only surprise is that it has taken God so long to vent his righteous anger on the sinner; still, he takes comfort in the deliciously incontrovertible fact that "Divine punishments, though slow, are always sure" (203). George Santayana said of the Puritan mentality that it thought it was beautiful that sin should exist so that it might be beautifully, inexorably punished. Thwackum's nose twitches eagerly at the hint of sin; he hunts sinners as Western hunts hares, with meditations full of birch, and his spiritual inheritor is Kafka's Whipper with his chilling claim: "I am here to whip."[6] At the novel's close he is as unteachable as ever, still preaching his infallible remedy for sin—scourging, still condemning Allworthy for the reprehensible lenity which allows vice to flourish. It is appropriate that, unlike Square, he does not repent. Square is, like Tartuffe, an impudent imposter, but Thwackum is the full-fledged Pharisee, the genuine article, who really does see himself as God's hit man—he is Alceste, a *self*-deceiver, a good man. What has a good man to repent who has done nothing wrong? Conversion in *Tom Jones* is apparently easier for the brazen atheist than for the convinced Christian—but, then, the devout were the most implacable foes of Jesus.

Thwackum as Pharisee knows the reason for Tom's broken arm: not a horse's hoof, but the hand of God. There is, for such a mentality, no mystery in suffering, no tragic, inexplicable incommensurability between the victim and his torment. On the contrary, all is as smoothly rational as a mathematical proof, as openly verifiable as a scientific experiment. Nothing is hidden, all is visibly ascertainable. Sinners suffer. If a man sins, expect the suffering; if a man suffers, seek the sin. That not only Pharisees are afflicted by this mania to turn pain into a science, to become actuaries of anguish by identifying the infallible, comforting system of cause and effect here as in the rest of the physical world, is shown by the question put to Jesus by his own disciples when they encountered the man blind from birth (John 9:1–5). Who, they demanded to know, was the sinner, the man or his parents, that he should be born blind? The sightless eyes prove guilt; all that remains is to identify the culprit.

In denying that anyone was guilty, man or parents, in rejecting altogether the relevance of guilt to the question, Jesus simultaneously attacked the assumption, axiomatic to Pharisee thought, that anguish belongs to the intelligible scientific world of cause and effect and that there is a logical explanation for pain; suffering is, rather, a mystery, not to be contained within the syllogisms and sorites of any rational system. The sufferer may be innocent, or, still more inexplicable, virtuous. When the healthy Thwackum tells the ailing Tom that sickness is the badge of sin, he is arrogantly proclaiming his own right to heaven while consigning Tom to hell. He is also advancing the basic arguments of Pharisaism: that the world is divided into saints and sinners, elect and reprobate, sheep and goats; that this division is visibly identifiable; and that the manifestly good have been commissioned by God to chastise the manifestly wicked. The moral mission of Jesus was to persuade us to abandon such pernicious beliefs. In *Tom Jones* we see Fielding waging the same campaign against the same enemies.

In this campaign Fielding's chief philosophical weapon is his insistence on a distinction between existence and essence, which thereby undermines the simplistic Pharisee reliance on external signs and appearances as the infallible index of God's favor or disapproval. The true judgment toward which Fielding summons us is a perilous activity, because in judging others we inevitably judge ourselves, a risk so complacently overlooked by arrogant Pharisaism. Fielding knows, no one better, how seduced our assessments can be by external appearances, how easily bribable our verdicts are by considerations of status and wealth (184). It is surprising, in view of his own essentially conservative temperament, that Fielding should so forcibly remind us how sin, or, more precisely, punishment for sin, is socially determined, dictated by class considerations. The candor of the Duchess of Buckingham's stinging rebuke to John Wesley makes this class animus splendidly clear: "It is monstrous to be told that you have a heart as sinful as the common wretches that crawl on the earth."[7] There speaks the voice of unabashed class Pharisaism. The Duchess is very willing to judge, but not to be judged. Sin is the prerogative of the lower orders, and the cultivated no more admitted its presence in their hearts than they did the canaille in their drawing rooms.

Fielding, from the privileged position as insider, scion of the aristocracy, warns us against such partisan bias. He knows how severe we are disposed to be on "whores in rags," how much more accommodating when the whores are wearing the latest Dior creations; and he challenges us to say what really offends us—the whores or the rags (445). Incarceration in Bridewell and being whipped at the cart's tail are for poor sinners like Molly; a rich sinner like Lady Bellaston will never suffer such a fate. Ironically, Fielding tells us that the otherwise ineffectual, indeed counterproductive, Bridewell inculcates at least one good lesson in those who suffer there: it teaches the poor to respect anew the gulf between the classes, because faults in them are punished there that are overlooked in their superiors (184). In another type of man such an insight might have instigated a demand for revolution, for the overthrow of an unjust society and the foundation of a new polity in which all were equal before the law, but Fielding is no revolutionary—it is a moral, individual reformation that he proposes, not a political and collective restructuring.

In any case, it goes much deeper than allowing our judgments to be swayed by the prestige of rank or wealth. The appearances that pervert true judgment may be more than the insignia of social status.

Deeds themselves may be a deception, totally misleading the onlooker as to the true inner worth of the actor. To be a good judge it is not enough to be good-natured or well-meaning; indispensable though these attributes be, they are necessary but not sufficient conditions of true judgment. One must be able to see through acts, to recognize that a chicken thief may be the Good Samaritan or that setting a bird at liberty may, in certain circumstances, be irrefutable proof of perfidy (*JA,* 70; *TJ,* 158). The good judge must be judicious, able to emancipate inner truth from surface appearance.

Central to this quality of judiciousness for Fielding is the need to be able to separate act and motive, deed and doer, and here the contrast with Swift is instructive. Swift, following the Baptist, insists on deeds as the sole reliable indicator of moral worth. A man is what he does—there is no spurious essence to defend us against an inculpating existence, no laudable inner self to which a man can legitimately appeal against the incriminating evidence of his actual behavior. A man is the sum of his actions and nothing else. Swift supplies a catalog of sordid, vicious habits as a description of how Yahoos behave; if, under oath, you are forced to confess these habits as your own, then you, too, are a Yahoo and there is no more to be said: *causa finita.* Fielding, far less rigorous, exhibits the generosity of a benevolent judge rather than the relentless pursuit of a Swiftian prosecutor. Not what a man *does* but what, at heart, he *is* is what counts. This consoling distinction between existence and essence is, as Coleridge notes, the defining characteristic of Fielding as moralist.[8]

The distinction has its Gospel source in Jesus' dismissal of the key Pharisee argument that decorum is the test of virtue, external observance the infallible proof of inner purity. The Pharisee declared that the godly man is he who follows certain rules and performs certain acts, while the reprobate is marked by his failure to do either: virtue is performance. Jesus countered by suggesting that performance is simply that, that a man who acts may be no more than an actor, a player—and Fielding reminds us that player and hypocrite are the same word in Greek (300). It follows that acts in themselves are not reliable indicators of vice or virtue: the ostensibly good man may be a sham, the apparent scoundrel a hero.

Fighting the Pharisees

Fielding insists against Swift that a man may fail himself in his actions, may libel his true essence, commit treason against his real self—a man, in short, may be better than his deeds. Deeds deceive. Tom Jones gets drunk and this is wrong, but a wise and compassionate judge (he cannot be one without the other) will consider the mitigating circumstances, the commendably ungovernable joy at Allworthy's miraculous recovery from seemingly imminent death. Blifil frees a bird from a cage not because he loves birds or freedom but because he hates Tom. Even had the bird escaped, Blifil would get no credit; that the poor creature is instantly devoured by a predator simply helps to illuminate the malice that freed it in the first place. For Swift and John the Baptist doing is the mirror of being; the filthy deeds of men reveal their rotten hearts, and they must repent, that is, act differently, or perish. Fielding and Jesus, less confident of the unerring testimony of acts, doubtful of Burke's assurance that conduct is the only language that never lies,[9] call for a profounder, more sympathetically intuitive assessment: a man may look guilty, like Tom or the publican, and be justified, while another, applauded for his goodness, may, like Blifil and the Pharisee, be in moral peril. Conduct can be as mendacious a language as any other. The distinction between existence and essence, deeds and nature, may be a consolation for the publican in the parable, Tom in the novel, and the accused sinner in general, but it has a contrary, an accusing and threatening import for Blifil and the tribe of Pharisees he represents.

Despite Coleridge's telling insight, it would, nevertheless, be a blunder to attribute to Fielding, of all men, an antinomian contempt for conduct. Far from upholding faith against works or slighting the importance of deeds, Fielding repeatedly stresses the indispensability of action, agreeing with Tillotson that "that man believes the gospel best who lives most according to it" (Rawson, 397); good living is for Fielding the soul of religion, with doctrinal purity trailing a long way behind. What might seem like an irresolvable contradiction in Fielding, a confusion as to the value, efficacy, or testimony of actions—on the one hand dismissing them as indicators of inner worth, on the other insisting that without them faith is empty—is once again unriddled with the help of the Gospels.

The contradiction between Jesus and the Baptist is more apparent than real. Superficially, it may seem that the Baptist upholds, while Jesus decries, the value of works; in truth, both regard action as crucial: we are *not* saved by faith alone, if by this is implied a disregard for deeds. Fielding's practical Christianity accords perfectly with Christ's warning that not the mouthers of the Father's name but the doers of the Father's will shall inherit the kingdom; in Fielding's secularized reprise the kingdom belongs to those who have good hearts, benevolent impulses, and actions to match. That the issue mattered greatly to Fielding is plain from its recurrence throughout his work. In *Joseph Andrews* he invites us to join him in condemning "the detestable doctrine of faith against good works"; in *Jonathan Wild* it is dragged in when Heartfree outrages the Newgate ordinary by arguing that a good pagan is more pleasing to God than a Christian rogue (*JA*, 70; *JW*, 165). Apart from rounding off the set of Heartfree's virtues, this has little to do with the plot, but that further serves to emphasize how large the theme bulked in Fielding's thought. It is not enough to *say* you believe; belief must be translated into action; otherwise you are the Baptist's dead branch, fit only for the fire.

Still, it would be hard to deny that, for Fielding, essence finally determines existence. Blifil, bad from birth, twisted in mind and nature, is incapable of a good action; what seems like one in such a man is pure illusion—it *must* be perverted at its root. What Calvin alleged against all men—that their seeming virtue is a mere skin over pollution, their good deeds simply a screen for corruption—is taken up and employed by Fielding against a certain type of man, of whom Blifil is his representative figure. Hence the paradox in Fielding: actions are *not* all-important when sundered from the hearts in which they are conceived and nurtured. Whatever he *does*, Blifil is rotten to the core. When Fielding ostentatiously refuses to make windows into Blifil, to journey into that heart of darkness—"it would be an ill office in us to pay a visit to the inmost recesses of his mind"—has not the visit, for all practical purposes, in the very moment of its renunciation, been devastatingly paid? (157). Do you need a tour of the whited sepulchre before you recognize how loathsome it is? (We shall see later how decisive this reticence is in determining Fielding's narrative mode, so antithetical to the prying intrusiveness favored by Richardson).

All of this, unarguably, is fully compatible with Christ's insistence that it is the heart, the motive, the desire, that finally determines the nature and quality of the deed. If the heart is Pharisaic, the deed, regardless of appearances, cannot be good. If Blifil frees a bird, seek the corruption; if he insists on telling the truth about Bridget's death to her dying brother, unearth the malice behind such murderous probity; if he pursues Sophia, not with fornication but with a respectable Christian marriage in mind, expose the sadistic perversion of his intent. What a man *is* must color what he does; the wicked soul can perform only wicked acts. How can a bad tree bear good fruit? All these acts—freeing a bird, telling the truth, courting a woman—may be good in themselves; but so, too, is going to the synagogue to pray. Everything depends upon the how and the why of its doing. So it seems obtuse to complain, as some readers do, that Blifil gets a raw deal simply because he lacks a good heart, or to advance as the chief argument on his behalf what is, in fact, the chief accusation against him. His heart *is* corrupt, his nature vicious. How did they become so? No more than Jesus does Fielding tell us how the Pharisee became a Pharisee; but, just as devastatingly as Jesus, he reveals the heap of bones strewn behind the gleaming facade.

Lest we risk missing this, Fielding, at the moment of Allworthy's final enlightenment, his insight into Blifil's perfidy, has him utter the explicit word of condemnation, the word chosen by Christ himself to denounce the Pharisees: "that wicked viper which I have so long nourished in my bosom" (845). Who can doubt that Blifil is here assuming his true place in a tradition of biblical obloquy that begins with the serpent of Eden and culminates in the vipers of Jesus? The source becomes completely unmistakable as Mrs. Miller, on her knees, prays the Christian prayer for the forgiveness of the adulterous woman, Mrs. Waters: "may Heaven shower down its choicest blessings upon her head, and for this one good action, forgive her all her sins be they never so many" (845). The very words of the Gospel are repeated in an eighteenth-century London drawing room; we might call it plagiarism but for the inescapable fact that Fielding so deliberately emblazons his "theft"; he wants us to detect it, to recognize in him the heir of Jesus, the foe of the Pharisees.

The novel exhibits the whole panoply of Pharisaism, with its parade of hypocrites representing every conceivable type, every possible subset: the immitigable villain posing as good man (Blifil), the sanctimonious frauds denouncing the sins they commit (Square, Bridget, Mrs. Wilkins), the sadist who really believes that his bloodlust is sanctioned by heaven (Thwackum). All, the villainous Blifil included, are comic, for reasons that will be examined in the final chapter, but the nature of the comedy, the categories of laughter, vary from one type to another.

In his onslaught on hypocrisy Fielding pioneers the mimetic style that Joyce was to bring to perfection in *Dubliners*. What at first glance seems like straight authorial reportage becomes, on inspection, an ironic dissection of the hypocrite trained in the narrator's sights. Bridget, we are told, cared so little for beauty (which she lacks) that she never mentioned it (54). Suspicions are aroused; the very proof offered of her contempt turns into its opposite—the suggestion that she indeed cared deeply about it and that the lack rankled badly. The case is clinched when we detect her obvious relish of the fact that so many beautiful women end up ruined, a speculation rounded off with a pharisaical acknowledgment to God for having so graciously exempted her from the odious gift: I thank thee, God, that I am not like other women—the prayer of the female Pharisee. The narrator pretends to find it strange that the ugliest women are the most circumspect, though the reader who knows his La Rochefoucauld will find no mystery there. Just as the trained bands eagerly present themselves for duty when there is no danger, so ugly women are punctiliously chaste because no man is interested—the women so keen on prudence do not need it.

The insight has an importance transcending the case in question. For example, it is contemptibly easy for men who have no way with women to attack Tom Jones for succumbing to temptation, yet only a charmer like Tom, overcoming the temptations so plentifully and readily offered, has a right to condemn Tom's indiscretions. Milton makes a similar point in the key argument of *Areopagitica*: only those who have been exposed to and solicited by temptation have ceased, morally speaking, to be children and may now be treated as moral beings;[10] conversely, there is something shamefully facile in pillorying the sins we are never likely to have a chance of committing. "By God, Mr. Chairman, at this moment I stand astonished at my own moderation."[11] Lord Clive, brought back from India to face charges of peculation in Parliament, implicitly challenges his accusers; those who have not been in his position are incapable of appreciating the modesty of his conduct, for the truly surprising thing is not his extortions but his abstentions. Similarly situated, what would his accusers have done?

Tom, had he been so minded, might have advanced a similar self-exculpation. Despite his reputation among critics as a squire of dames, Tom is really a naïf where women are concerned, comically deluding himself that he is pursuer and seducer when he is really the prey. In any case, balancing his three lapses (with Molly, Mrs. Waters, and Lady Bellaston) are the three victories he wins in the final section of the novel: the rebuff of the sexual advances of Mrs. Fitzpatrick; the refusal of Mrs. Waters's sexual gambits on her prison visit; and, most heroic of all, considering his penniless condition consequent on abandoning Lady Bellaston, added to the apparently irrecoverable loss of Sophia, his rejection of the young, rich, and pretty widow Mrs. Hunt in her offer of honorable, profitable marriage (773, 811, 735). If only those capable of Tom's abstentions were to attack him, the number of his condemners would be much reduced.

Fielding's earlier ironic exposure of Bridget's hypocrisy warns those who condemn Tom, whether character or reader, to be scrupulously honest in scrutinizing their motives; envy of the successful philanderer, chagrin at one's own sexual incompetence, may so easily be alchemized into a spurious moral indignation. It is Christ's recurring charge against the Pharisees: their seeming virtue, forever expressing itself in the indictment of others, masks an inner corruption. Fielding similarly insists that the condemnation of sinners is not necessarily a proof of virtue. Who is more likely to chastise Tom's monetary recklessness than the avaricious Blifil, who more zealous to expose his drunkenness than his strategically abstemious adversary, who more eager to pillory his imprudent though healthy sexuality than the pervert who dreams not of love, nor even of sex, but only of violation? The accuser is not necessarily holy: it is Fielding's key ethical insight, as it is also Christ's. "That higher order of women," so avid to condemn their frailer sisters, may well be impelled by envy and chagrin. By the time the narrator tells us that these touchy women are severely left alone by men—"from despair, I suppose, of success"—his cheek is fairly bulging with his tongue, and the cause of their touchiness not hard to infer (54). How easy it is to parade necessity as a virtue, to alchemize incapacity into merit, or to elevate spite into principle! On this topic Fielding has nothing to learn from Nietzsche. With Fielding in the vicinity there is no chance of perpetrating such a fraud; like a moral weights-and-measures man, he may at any moment arrive with his true scales to verify the standards we habitually employ. It is the hypocrite-trader who has most to fear.

Allworthy's housekeeper, among the first of the frauds to be exposed, is clearly a cheat of this kind. Finding the child in his bed, Allworthy rings for the elderly Mrs. Wilkins, but is so engaged with the infant, so oblivious of self, that he forgets he is undressed. But Mrs. Wilkins is not forgetful of self. Here, Fielding insinuates, is the crude reality behind the tense Richardsonian myth of imperiled female servants and lustful masters, the truth underlying the fantasy of procrastinated rape on which Fielding's great rival had based his work and built his reputation. The contrast is between the abstracted man, so absorbed with the discovery of the foundling child that he forgets he is in his shirt (the eighteenth-century euphemism for naked), and the shrewd, calculating woman, her mind concentrated on how she can turn a nocturnal summons to her master's bedroom to her own material advantage. Paradoxically, the scandalously naked man is a paragon of virtue, while the respectably clothed matron is a sexual schemer, who, summoned in the night, first visits her mirror, not to make herself decent but seductive, not to conceal but to advertise her charms. That Mrs. Wilkins is not a nubile young charmer like Pamela simply makes her vamping ambitions more risible, but not less reprehensible. Her failure is not to her credit; she is still a scheming female, though laughably without a hope of success, a joke who tried to be a threat. She finds her master as she hopes—naked—and her strategic swoon, in the best Pamela tradition, could only have facilitated the sexual onslaught she anticipates, had her innocent employer ever entertained any such desires (56).

Overcoming the disappointment of her master's sexual indifference, she immediately exhibits that salient trait of Pharisaism, the lust to punish. Not the child's welfare but the mother's chastisement is her first thought. Transplant her to New England and she will easily take her place among those demanding harsher penalties for Hester Prynne; transplant her to the Palestine of Christ and she will be strong for the stoning of the adulteress. Her mind hankers after punishment—Bridewell and the cart's tail—no whipping being too severe for such sluts, especially one who has so patently tried to incriminate Allworthy. Allworthy is astonished at the observation. For a magistrate he seems curiously naive, quaintly assuming, in advance of Kafka's Joseph K., that only guilty men are accused. The more knowing Mrs. Wilkins reminds him that "the world is censorious," but it is a world projected from her own suspicious mentality and made in her own image; she is the scandalmonger (57). Fortunately for Tom, Allworthy rejects the role of Laius that Mrs. Wilkins would have him play—the "father" threatened by an infant son who deals with the threat through infanticide. Here, as at the climax of the novel, Tom is, at worst, a comic Oedipus, which is to say a false Oedipus, a *not*-Oedipus, entirely appropriate in a work that is a Christian comedy rather than a pagan tragedy.

The housekeeper's attitude toward the child is reminiscent of Gulliver's toward the Yahoo infant: "it goes against me to touch these misbegotten wretches, whom I don't look upon as my fellow creatures. Faugh, how it stinks! It doth not smell like a Christian" (57). The absurdity of the complaint (do Christian babies come toilet-trained?) should not mask the malice or the consciousness of difference, of superiority, which is the Pharisee's hallmark; this same sense of election inspires her brutal solution of the problem. She is for wrapping the child in a basket and leaving it on the highway; the odds are about two to one in favor of survival till morning, but, even should it die, it will be for the best, since, in the idiom of the *Modest Proposal,* what future happiness can there be for such a misbegotten wretch? This is funny, but in the way that Swift or Joe Orton is funny: there is savagery in the humor.

In the parade of the Pharisees, Mrs. Wilkins, in addition to being the first of the punishers, hence the first contributor to a key debate in the novel that will continue almost to the last page, is also the first of those who prophesy a disastrous finale for Tom. But for the moment his is not to be the fate of Oedipus; when the unheeding Allworthy commands that, rather than be exposed to the elements, the child is to be cared for, the timeserver at once switches and plays the third of a series of rapidly assumed roles, that of the motherly woman following on outraged moralist and shocked maiden. Forgetting her recent abhorrence, she takes the child, the "sweet little infant" (somehow miraculously freshened), into her arms—a testimony less to her capacity for conversion than to a shrewd awareness of the dangers of defying an employer (58). Mrs. Wilkins lacks the courage of her odious convictions; she can pretend love for a Yahoo child provided it pays to do so. Like the lawyer in *Joseph Andrews* who insists, for purely selfish reasons, on caring for the injured man (*JA*, 69), Mrs. Wilkins is still wrong even when she does right, supplying yet another instance of Eliot's greatest treason.

Once again Fielding exhorts us to search behind the deed for the all-decisive motive. Tom will turn out to be the opposite of the timeserving housekeeper, because he does the wrong deed for the right reason: telling a lie to save Black George, getting drunk to celebrate his benefactor's recovery, while Blifil, his uncle's would-be killer, sits discreet and sober, harvesting all the false credit of an outward decorum. Throughout the entire scene between Allworthy and Mrs. Wilkins we have an exposure of the doublethink that Fielding tended to associate with the basic Richardsonian situation of beleaguered maiden and rampant rapist; the man is naked not because he is lasciv-

ious but because he is virtuous; the woman, epitome of outward re-
spectability, is obsessed by thoughts of self.

These same thoughts of self are clearly visible in Fielding's reprise
of the parable of the laborers in the vineyard, the deathbed declaration
of Allworthy's will. The metaphor of the indignant laborers who feel
they have been bilked by the boss coalesces with the repulsive image
in St. Matthew of the vultures gathering round the corpse (Matt.
20:1–16; 24:28) to shape Fielding's description of the bogus deathbed
scene in which the household assembles to hear Allworthy's bequests.
However dissimilar laborers and vultures are, they are linked by a
rapacious resolve to grab as much as they can get. When the vulture
has been schooled by Pharisees, it is also convinced that its deserts are
greater than its share.

Only by recognizing its parable origin will we be prevented from
misconstruing this episode. After Allworthy's recovery, the narrator
informs us that the illness had never been so serious as what the doctor
diagnosed (233, 225). But we would be wrong to conclude that we
are dealing with a hypochondriac and an inept doctor, because the
latter decides and the former believes that death is imminent; far from
being a hypochondriac, Allworthy tends to neglect himself, while the
fact that the doctor confuses a bad cold with incipient rigor mortis is
not, in this context, necessarily a proof of folly. Quite apart from the
fact that the plot requires Allworthy to be unavailable when the lawyer Dowling calls, Fielding needs a deathbed to develop another aspect
of his theme, the debunking of Pharisaism. We are at this point reading
a parable, not a psychologically realistic fiction. Parable will not tol-
erate too strict a psychological scrutiny, is discomfited when we ask it
too many specific and particularized questions. Where did the woman
get the precious jar of ointment? No matter, it is what she did with it
that counts. Why was the man who sowed tares in the corn the farm-
er's enemy? Could it be that he had cause, or was at least mitigated,
in seeking revenge? These are misguided speculations, as totally out
of place here as they would be appropriate to realistic fiction. In this
parable of the field we simply have the datum, not the explanation, of
enmity; all else is irrelevant to the story's understanding. Christ's only

interest is in the practical problem: Now that the field *is* in such a condition, what are we to do with it? The parameters of parable are strict, and this holds equally for Fielding's bogus deathbed scene. We are not meant to speculate about hypochondria or the medical incompetence that mistakes a snuffle for the death rattle. Fielding needs a deathbed (better in a comedy that it should be bogus) so that he can display certain attributes of human nature: cupidity, resentment, envy, sense of injured merit, and so on. His only aim is to lay bare the rancor and disgruntlement of the beneficiaries, the laborers in Allworthy's vineyard.

Allworthy does not fear death. If a pagan like Cato could despise it, how much more easily can a Christian fortified by the infinitely superior promises of his religion do so. He likens his approaching death to that of a faithful laborer at harvest end, summoned to receive his reward from a bountiful master—a splendidly appropriate prelude to the modern rendition of the parable that follows (225–26). Allworthy, too, is a bountiful master and has gathered his friends for the final comfort of witnessing their satisfaction at the legacies provided. He is, of course, yet again woefully mistaken. Only Tom and Blifil are unresentful. Tom, grief-stricken at the approaching death, is heedless of legacies. Blifil *is* satisfied with the fortune left him, so satisfied, indeed, that he tries to hasten the benefactor's demise by communicating, against the doctor's advice, the sad news of Bridget's passing, using his own mother's death as a means of killing off his uncle.

Everyone else—Mrs. Wilkins, Thwackum, Square—is angry and discontented, each resenting the other's share, each convinced that he or she has been cheated. All shed, of course, the tears obligatory on such occasions (229)—when was a Pharisee ever found wanting in ritual exactitude? But this is rote mourning, mere eye-service. That Fielding is not the naive Polyanna, the Shaftesburian simpleton, invented by some critics, optimistically viewing human nature through the rosiest-tinted glasses, is shown in the chapter heading: "Containing matter rather natural than pleasing"(229). The resentment of the rancorous Pharisees is, regrettably, a natural reaction, not some monstrous aberration of ingratitude imported from another species on another planet. Mrs. Wilkins fumes privately against her employer's failure to reward her own superior merit: "now we are all put in a lump together"(230)—precisely the complaint of the disgruntled laborers, made all the more outrageously comic in the light of her self-confessed peculations, the fact that, like the unjust steward, she has been robbing her master for years.

Both she and the similarly disappointed Thwackum comfort themselves in the standard way of envious Pharisaism: their enemy, who is ipso facto God's enemy too, is headed for hell—"he is now going where he must pay for all" (230). The narcissism of the Pharisee is comically yet arrestingly manifested, not merely in the relish of another's everlasting torment, but also in the notion that God will send Allworthy to hell for not giving Thwackum more money. It is not so much having God in your corner as having him in your pocket. Small wonder that they concur so readily with Blifil's resolve to tell the "dying" man the sad news of his sister's death; those who condemn you to hell will scarcely shrink from condemning you to death. That Blifil can hypocritically cite obedience and truth as justifying his disclosure merely highlights the Pharisaism, because here obedience is the sin and truth a means of murder (232). Even without knowing Blifil's malicious motive—and quite apart from the stunning dishonesty of pleading truth while withholding from his uncle the greatest truth of all, that of Tom's parentage (withheld on a first reading, be it noted, not only from Allworthy but also from the reader)—the sensible argument against such formulaic rigidity is that circumstances alter cases, that one must always take the context into account. Should a man in danger of dying be told bad news? Is truth an idol to which everything else must be sacrificed? Accused of desecrating the Sabbath, Jesus retorted that the Son of Man is lord of the Sabbath, thereby upholding human love and need against an inflexible, inhuman code. Even were his reverence for truth genuine, Blifil would still stand convicted; that it is merely a mask for murder exposes him as a monster.

It is one of the triumphs of Fielding's art that even a monster like Blifil should finally be seen as comic, or, at least, should easily and without any sense of strain take his position within the total comic structure of the work. A character like Square provides a very different kind of comedy and provokes a very different brand of laughter. Why do we laugh at Square? The preface to *Joseph Andrews* will tell us: "To discover any one to be the exact reverse of what he affects" is, says Fielding, the essence of the ridiculous (*JA*, 29), and Square is the foremost example of the ridiculous in *Tom Jones*. When the Pharisee is caught with his trousers down, he is comic, especially when the debagging reveals a man who is just the same as other men. We laugh because Fielding contrives through his art that we must. Note the obvious relish of the narrator in the "wicked" rug that fell and left the shivering philosopher exposed (215). The normal, straightforward, moral explication of the transferred epithet would be that the rug is wicked because it *hid* the wrongdoer, but here the narrator ironically condemns it for *ceasing* to hide him. The narrator may say "unhappily," but he is clearly overjoyed that the rug fell—all the more so if Molly, in her simulated rage as she plays the role of betrayed maiden, really did unintentionally displace it; God's ways are wonderful indeed—would it not be deliciously apt if she *acted* herself into her predicament?

"With shame I write it, and with sorrow will it be read" (215); but we know there is nothing of the kind, on both counts. For shame substitute elation, for sorrow, delight. As the rug falls the narrator describes how the "philosopher" Square (just in case the reader has forgotten his vocation) is crouched, in the position of a soldier punished by being tied neck to heel, or of a miscreant disgustingly excreting in the public street, "among *other* female utensils" (215). It is the linking of "philosopher" and "other" that does all the comic damage; the pretentious self-elevated man is revealed with as much dignity as a dildo or a jordan. The spectacle of his large, staring eyes gazing from beneath Molly's nightcap would be risible enough in any man; in the philosopher it is sidesplitting. In *The Mechanical Operation of the Spirit* Swift ridicules the philosophic claim to have raised the soul above matter, and nominates the unfortunate Thales as the archetype of those philosophic blunderers. Walking along, his eyes fixed dreamily on the stars, he falls into a ditch, a slimy hole in the earth, the appropriate nemesis of such abstracted visionaries.[12] Square, unlike

Thales, is simply a fraud, and the manner of his exposure makes it impossible, as the narrator says, for any spectator to refrain from "immoderate laughter" (215).

Such laughter is the revenge of reality on phony aspiration, of life on pretension. The wise and grave man, normally preening himself on his pedestal, is found skulking shamefaced in Molly's bedroom, and the hoot of comic incongruity that erupts comes from the perception that the wise and grave man is no different from you and me. Square is not being ridiculed for being a sexual creature, but for pretending *not* to be a sexual creature, for posing as superior to other men. Not the fornicator but the Pharisee is targeted; his present behavior is natural enough, it is his previous rhetoric that is intolerable. "Philosophers are composed of flesh and blood as well as other people" (216): only let *them* remember this and there will be no need for *us* to remind them. If they are superior at all, it is in theory, not practice; their speculations may be more refined than ours, but their conduct is no different.

The inescapable question presents itself: why does Fielding find it funny? Why is he not more incensed against the hypocrite? Is this yet further evidence of what some critics regard as a laxity or compliance, a too ready indulgence toward sin, in Fielding himself? Fielding might well have posed a counterquestion: what is there to get angry about? Why rage against nature? Had Square been honest with us from the start about his natural impulses, the case against him would scarcely be worth pursuing. We are all in the same fallible boat, all sons of Adam; even the gravest of men may sometimes stoop to reading certain books and looking at certain pictures. This genial forbearance in Fielding is, after all, an essential element in all comedy; it is the arrogant, the rigorous, the overstrict who are the targets of leveling comedy, which seeks to bring them down to their proper place alongside ordinary mortals. Comic nemesis invariably attends comic hubris. The Duke in *Measure for Measure* may talk contemptuously of love, but he will end up a married man for all that. Not what Square does but rather the secrecy with which he does it—this is Fielding's target and he merrily takes aim.

Where Jesus gets angry at the hypocrite, Fielding is amused; Jesus finds no mirth in sin, Fielding forever unearths comedy. What Square says to Tom—"I see you enjoy this mighty discovery and—taste great delight in the thoughts of exposing me" (218)—might be even more appropriately directed at Fielding himself. Far from shaking his head over Square's deplorable behavior, Fielding enjoys it immensely: "I was never better pleased with thee in my life"; the reader senses a second, authorial voice here reinforcing and echoing Tom's words (219). Tom has, of course, a personal stake in Square's humiliating exposure—it gets him off a very difficult moral hook with Molly; but even allowing for this selfish interest, there is a patently uncensorious note in this, a live-and-let-live attitude. Tom *is* pleased at the discovery for selfish reasons, but he is also pleased to find Square for once behaving like a man instead of a philosophic calculating machine. It is, admittedly, splendidly convenient; nevertheless, Fielding does not cheat—there is no manipulation of puppets to provide Tom with an easy escape. Square *is* a fraud, Molly a trollop; they act according to their natures, predictably, consistently, as we can see in retrospect, and the scene ends not just with Tom happy but with everybody happy: a genial conclusion from a genial narrator.

It is this genial temperament that makes Fielding unsympathetic to any form of Pharisaism, including that curious type that assumes its superiority, not to others, but to itself, claiming an immunity from nature, a status out of this world. Fielding has been faulted for his tolerance of sinners; he is, we are told, too good-humored for indignation, too pleased with life to demand reform.[13] "Ye must be perfect even as your Father in heaven is perfect": the exhortation is inconceivable in Fielding's mouth. Indeed, he cautions us against the itch for perfection as ruinous to social intercourse and self-repose: "Men of true wisdom and goodness are contented to take persons and things as they are, without complaining of their imperfections, or attempting to amend them" (112). Let ill alone, advises Fielding, rest easy in reality instead of hankering after some impossible utopia. It is good advice, even for villains; if Blifil had not schemed to ruin Tom, he would have ended up as Allworthy's heir.

The personal note is unmistakable as the narrator tells us that he requires the kind of friend who both sees and overlooks faults, and assures us of his own readiness to reciprocate: "Forgiveness . . . we give and demand in turn" (112). Echoes of the Lord's Prayer are easily audible in Fielding's definition of a friend: someone who forgives. Will the God who made us be any less generous, less friendly? Fielding comes close to anticipating Heine: "*Dieu me pardonnera—c'est son métier.*" Conversely, "there is, perhaps, no surer mark of folly, than an attempt to correct the natural infirmities of those we love" (113), as the perfectionist zealot of Hawthorne's *The Birthmark* so tragically learns. As with the finest china, so with the best of men: in each may be an incurable flaw; but what witlessness to discard either for the sake of one defect. And how can what would be folly in man become wisdom in God? He, too, loves us as we are and is not so unreasonable as to demand an unprocurable faultlessness. Fielding's God predictably resembles Fielding.

The rigorous moralist may command us to sin no more; Fielding is content if our failings should be no worse than flesh is heir to. Pascal, pondering with bemused indignation the human penchant for diversion,[14] would have identified Western's sudden forgetting of his beloved runaway daughter to go chasing after a fox as another instance of this reprehensible distraction in man, this zany inability to concentrate upon what really matters; Fielding relishes the eccentricity too much to censure his madcap squire; the author-God loves Western too much to wish him changed (555). The humorist evicts the moralist.

Man is what he is, whatever fools and fanatics say. Even grief must eat at last; Fielding offers this as a fact, not as a stricture (748). What for Orwell in *Nineteen Eighty-four* is a source of anguish—the fact that the aspiring spirit is demeaningly shackled to a subversively feeble body—is accepted by Fielding with cheerful good humor. Contemplating Tom at Upton, Fielding lightheartedly tells us that heroes, self-esteem and the world's adulation notwithstanding, are finally mere flesh and blood: "However elevated their minds may be, their bodies at least (which is much the major part of most) are liable to the worst infirmities, and subject to the vilest offices of human nature"

(453). There is no hint here of Paul's anguished prayer to be delivered from the body of this death. Heroes and philosophers have bellies and genitals like other men, and these organs require a like satisfaction as in lesser mortals: "To say the truth, as no known inhabitant of this globe is really more than man, so none need be ashamed of submitting to what the necessities of man demand"(453). No one is excluded from this general amnesty. Fielding adumbrates Brecht's *erst essen*, though in a very different sense; only after he has satisfied his hunger does Tom think of sex. The lady is no more to blame than the hero. Tom is an irresistible combination of Hercules and Adonis, and has, if more were needed, just saved her life. Only a prude will blame her for falling for so attractive a champion.

Fielding's indulgence toward his erring characters reaches its Everest point in an especially audacious piece of special pleading, when, employing the metaphor of love as feast, he tells us that Mrs. Waters is not too "nice," that is, squeamish or scrupulous, to dine where she knows that someone else has a prior claim, or has, indeed, dined previously—her suspicion that Tom loves someone else does not prevent her present enjoyment. This, the narrator concedes, may not be as refined as we might wish, but it is at least more wholesome and less spiteful than the niggardly attitude of those ascetic females who will happily forego enjoying their lovers provided no one else does. We are, presumably, to prefer Mrs. Waters's sexual largesse, her openhearted spirit, to the spiteful hoarding of a puritanism that denies the self and everyone else (461). It would, of course, be completely unreasonable to blame Fielding for not anticipating AIDS and the possibly catastrophic consequences of Mrs. Waters's generosity today; but neither, from our ambiguously privileged position, can we regard such promiscuity with the same casual indulgence as Fielding. Morally, we may still agree with him; medically, we cannot.

In fairness to Fielding, it should be said that he is *not* the irresponsible advocate of a sexual free-for-all. Tom, admittedly, seems to open the door to this in his perhaps too ready palliation of Square: "what can be more innocent than the indulgence of a natural appetite?" (218). Still, he takes a very different line in his stern rebuke to Nightingale over his treatment of Nancy (668), and Allworthy, surely not here Fielding's butt, has at the start of the novel denounced "the vice of incontinence" (186). Yet most readers will surely rise from *Tom Jones* feeling that we are too obsessed with sexual weaknesses, exaggerating their importance in the graph of human imperfection, often condemning as wicked or sinful what is simply a datum of life, an inescapable fact of experience—or, at least, that this is what the author *wants* us to feel. It has to do with the revaluation of values, the restructuring of the league-table of sins, that we shall examine in the next chapter. Consider the narrator's comment on Tom's inability to resist the temptation to snatch a glance at Mrs. Waters's splendid breasts—what reader, whatever his own views on the matter, believes that Fielding condemns this as sinful rather than accepting it as natural? (444).

So the general point about Fielding's tolerance is valid. Swift's truth about man is intended to shame us, Fielding's to deliver us from shame. We must not scourge ourselves for what is trivial or unavoidable; we must live at peace within the limitations of the body, refusing to allow the aberrations of an extravagant Platonism to impose upon us, always remembering our first fealty to flesh and blood. Blood is thicker than Platonism. Depressed at Sophia's resolve never to marry against her father's will, Tom is, nevertheless, comforted to read in the same letter that she will just as surely not be coerced into an unappealing marriage. No man is so incredibly exalted, so much an enthusiast of love, as to wish his mistress married to another, even if this marriage were to make her completely happy. Such selfless devotion, if it exists at all, must be "a gift confined to the female part of the creation"; certainly, the narrator has heard only women claiming to possess it, "though I cannot pretend to say, I have ever seen an instance of it" (756). Do women exceed men in love—or is it simply that men exceed women in honesty? To tell such a truth shames only the devil, not the self. It is this calm, unextravagant fidelity to fact that identifies Fielding as the ancestor of Jane Austen, as witness Emma's sensible refusal to allow any "flight of generosity run mad" to enter her brain.[15]

Fielding no more approves of self-deceivers than he does of outright cheats: each is the foe of truth. Take Tom's thicket adventure with Molly: "With sorrow we relate, and with sorrow, doubtless, will it be read" (238)—but the historian must tell truth, however distressing or unpleasant. So Fielding begins the chapter in which the drunken Tom, dreaming of Sophia and swearing eternal constancy to her, ends up copulating in the bushes with Molly. It echoes an earlier irony as Fielding zestfully prepares to pull the rug away from Square: "with shame I write it, and with sorrow will it be read"—but there are crucial differences. Square plots like a boudoir Napoleon the seduction of Molly; all goes according to plan until Tom's unexpected visit and the accident of the rug. Moreover, Square has not only posed as the Stoic wise man, apathetically superior to appetite, but has implacably condemned Tom for his shameful surrender to passion. Hence the reader, far from repining, is delighted to discover the sham behind the rug—Square, too good to be true, gets his thoroughly deserved comeuppance. Far from shame and sorrow, the reader shares the narrator's joy in the unmasking.

Tom's self-deception is of a less flagrant kind. Love, says Woody Allen, is the answer, but while we are waiting for the answer, sex can raise some pretty interesting questions. Such opportunism does not really fit the case of the drunken, surprised Tom, taken almost unawares amid his ecstatic protestations. Tom, drunk and vulnerable, has not reckoned on meeting an avid Molly. The target is not so much his conduct after Molly's arrival as his rhetoric before it. Should any man, never mind one as drunk and unguarded as Tom, so recklessly give such verbal hostages to fortune? As always in Fielding, comic nemesis waits in the wings. As background, Fielding supplies all the stock software of conventional pastoral romance—grove, stream, nightingale, smitten lover. Tom is exalted—and also inebriated and irresponsible. In the earlier exposure scene, the consciously hypocritical Molly, her new lover still hidden behind the rug, declaims like a tragic heroine: "I can never love any other man as long as I live" (215). Tom, less consciously culpable, is a self-deceiver: "But why do I mention another woman?" (239). To which the short, ironic answer is: because Molly is just around the corner. As Tom, in the throes of an absurdly hyperbolic devotion, vows to tear out his eyes rather than look at another woman, there are echoes not only of a comic Oedipus but of an inappropriate Gospel: if thine eye offends thee, pluck it out.

But in comedy men are no better than men and self-mutilation is out of place; all Tom's high-flown protestations end laughably with the hero leading Molly into the thicket. Know thyself: the treasure of pagan wisdom is not to be despised by the Christian hero.

To know oneself: is there a more exacting moral and intellectual discipline? Of all writers Fielding is most acutely aware of how deep-seated, perhaps ineradicable, is the human talent for self-deception. A hypocrite is someone who. . . . But who isn't? So pervasive is the malady that even the good characters seem occasionally at risk of lapsing into pharisaical self-esteem. Does not our first view of the good Mr. Allworthy provoke a certain unease, however slight or qualified? "A human being replete with benevolence, meditating in what manner he might render himself most acceptable to his Creator, by doing most good to his creatures" (59). Is it not just a trifle lush, excessive, a shade too programmatic and self-conscious? Tom, in the first flush of his heroic resolve to sacrifice himself rather than pursue Sophia to her ruin, is temporarily suffused with a glow of self-congratulation and pride in his own achievement, though the reality of loss quickly reasserts itself and conceit withers (289). Sophia herself is not above the insidious seductions of self-flattery. She is tempted to obey her father's command to marry Blifil from motives of duty and religion, but also from the "agreeable tickling in a certain little passion," neither religious nor virtuous in itself, but often acting as the auxiliary of both (329). Had not Mandeville scandalously and subversively proposed that virtue is mere vanity?[16] Hypocrisy is, it seems, a pit into which anyone can fall.

It is therefore, deliciously surprising and artistically superb that Fielding should end his onslaught on hypocrisy (for, morally, that is what *Tom Jones* is) with an instance at once innocent and delightful, as Sophia, in docile submission to her father's will, meekly agrees to marry the man for whom she yearns. Thy will be done, says the obedient handmaid of the Lord. What splendid consummation when duty and desire are one, and obedience is self-gratification. *E'n la sua volontade è nostra pace.*[17] To love the Lord's commands: it is, with the Virgin as archetype and model, the highest aspiration of the Christian soul.

5

Judging the Jurors

Not the standard alignment with Richardson but the contrast with Swift is the more fruitful way to begin assessing Fielding. The difference between the two satirists is revealed in the very diverse ways they treat their readers, even to the contrasting modes of address. Where Gulliver speaks placatingly to the gentle reader, Fielding's narrator appeals directly to the judicious reader.[1] Swift forever sets traps for his prime enemy, the reader, who, perhaps complacently, certainly with no prior knowledge of the threat to himself, innocently turns the pages of the "Voyage to the Houyhnhnms" or the *Modest Proposal* or the *Argument Against Abolishing Christianity.* We stroll into Swift's courtroom, serenely unaware of the charges against us; we exit shaken and condemned, vainly protesting that we are not Yahoos, but the victims of some chill miscarriage of justice, some tragic case of mistaken identity.

With Fielding we find ourselves in a very different courtroom with a very different judge. In *Tom Jones* there are tests rather than traps, and there is an absence of that hidden malice toward the reader which is so frighteningly found in Swift. Instead, there is a challenge, sincere and direct. If Fielding's novels, like Swift's satires, read us rather than we them, it is nevertheless in a radically different, much less demoralizing way. Swift strives to humiliate, to drive us from our intolerable pride toward a chastened admission of guilt—the only fitting response to the accusation, "thou art the man." Our dismay springs from the shock of finding ourselves in the dock, when all along, like David, we presumed we were listening to someone else's story. Fielding, by contrast (with certain crucial tactical exceptions to be discussed later), undeviously invites us to be jurors; there is a case to be settled, a problem solved, and Fielding genuinely seeks the reader's support in directing him toward a conclusion already reached by the magisterial author.

If we blunder in Swift and go incriminatingly astray, that is all according to the satiric plan, for it is we who are on trial and Swift is our accuser. And so he continually leads us on, tempting us into agreements that will later be used damagingly against us. At certain points in this satire—the "Digression on Madness," the climax of the fourth voyage, the disavowal of primitive Christianity as beyond any reasonable defense or possible recall—the reader is shockingly left treading air, desperately seeking a toehold anywhere, bewilderingly aware that he has been betrayed where he most trusted, above all, still agonizingly in the dark as to why this has happened to him: Why has the friend proved so false?

Betrayal is Swift's business; he is the master of literary entrapment. If we blunder in Fielding (the aforementioned exceptions apart—and even here, as we shall see, the aim is humility, not humiliation), we do so against his wishes, for he has no design to incriminate us. He wants us to share his view of Parson Adams and Tom Jones, of the transported postilion and "the detestable doctrine of faith against good works," and of all the other judicial problems that surface in his court; the hope is that we will pass, not fail, the tests (*JA*, 70, 93). Fielding needs us for jury service; if we end up in the dock instead, the fault is entirely ours. Swift despises the reader and contemptuously spurns the offer of alliance: "I damn such Fools!—Go, go, you're bit." How dare we presume to agree? Hence the recurring problem throughout Swift of anguishing over meaning when the author deliberately frustrates agreement, confounds judgment. His greatest artistic pleasure is to drive the reader toward impasse, snaring him between equally unacceptable alternatives—cannibalism or justice for Ireland, fool or knave, Gulliver as sage or gull, Christianity as sorry compromise or utopian ideal—with all egress barred toward any other solution. The God who presides over Fielding's fiction has nothing in common with the vengeful practical joker of "The Day of Judgement."[2]

Fielding, in sharp contrast to Swift, tries to recruit the reader as friend and ally, so much so that from the beginning critics have objected to these efforts of the author to intrude himself into his fiction. "I think, I can with less pains write one of the books of this history, than the prefatory chapter to each of them" (739). A number of critics (thankfully diminishing as Fielding's art is better appreciated, more deeply discerned) have regretted that he ever gave himself such pains at all, clearly believing that *Tom Jones* would be a better novel by a better novelist if the authorial comments, interpolations, directions, intrusions were wholly removed. Lord Monboddo was a pioneer in blaming Fielding for gate-crashing his own novels, indiscreetly turning up where he has no right to be (Rawson, 177–78). Sir Walter Scott begins by agreeing, but changes his mind in pronouncing these chapters of authorial intervention the most entertaining in the book.[3] Today, despite the fairly recent complaints of Madox Ford (Rawson, 353) and others, the narrator is generally recognized as being the most important character in Fielding's work. Clearly, those who resent the interventions are objecting to a vital element in Fielding's art.

This, if anything, is understating their significance. The fact that Fielding went on subjecting himself to the pains of their composition is sufficient testimony to the importance *he* attached to these offending chapters—and rightly so. Those who favor the excisions are, without realizing or intending it, emasculating Fielding, castrating the work and condescending to the art. Milan Kundera approvingly repeats Hermann Broch's dictum that the sole raison d'être of a novel is to discover what only the novel can discover, and goes on to speculate that the novel is Europe's creation and that the *sequence of discoveries* (not the sum of what was written) is what constitutes the history of the European novel: "It is only in such a supranational context that the value of a work (that is to say the import of its discovery) can be fully seen and understood."[4] There is a fanciful yet attractive suggestion of the European novel as one great waterway with a number of eminent novelists flowing like tributaries into it. If Fielding takes his deserved place alongside these other masters, it is largely because of the discoveries made in these introductory chapters and in the entire narrative methodology predicated on them. *Tom Jones* discovers what only it can by virtue of these prefaces; pointing to them, Fielding might with equal justice have anticipated the words of Gerard Manley Hopkins's God-praiser: "What I do is me: for that I came."[5]

They are not *a* vital element but *the* vital element of the work. In a book that is about the importance of reading, interrogating us as to the kind of readers we are, indeed going so far as to assert that *how* you read reveals and determines *who* you are, the introductory chapters are vital, indispensable. Fielding's novel investigates the role of the reader as well as recounting the foundling's adventures. We are advised that the novelists of the period were interested in exploring different ways of relating to their readers, and that, far from attempting to disguise it, they incorporated this interest in their novels.[6] Fielding, clearly, was as much concerned to shape a reader as to form a fiction, to create not just a story but a reader for that story, one who—and the phrase, as we shall see, is crucial—would do it justice.

In the introduction to book 7, "A Comparison between the World and the Stage," Fielding's surprising variation on a threadbare theme is to switch attention from stage to auditorium, away from the handful of players treading the boards to the mass of actors thronging the theater, in gallery, stalls, and boxes. Everyone in the building is a player, not just those in possession of equity cards. The same insight informs his novel. There are judgments and judges within *Tom Jones* (the book is crowded with them), but the most important judges of all are its readers, situated outside the text. In reading the book, in judging the characters, we read and judge ourselves, just as surely as Mrs. Wilkins betrays her own censorious heart when she calls Allworthy's attention to the censorious world—the book reads us as we read it. In one of the most remarkable reversals in fiction, in an astonishing reflex, the jurors discover themselves being judged. The case of David is perhaps not so inapposite to Fielding as was first suggested. This chapter attempts to demonstrate the qualified sense in which such an indictment of the reader, or, more precisely, of a certain kind of reader, occurs in *Tom Jones*.

That Fielding was acutely conscious of the innovative, indeed revolutionary, nature of his work needs no arguing: it is palpable in his own reiterated claims, but even more so in his striving to establish a relationship between narrator-judge and reader-juror. The prefaces are crucial in this process of definition. When, in a series of changing metaphors, Fielding seeks the definitive image of this relationship, there is a foreshadowing of Freud straining to expound the new discipline of psychoanalysis: "In psychology we can describe only with the help of comparisons. . . . But we are forced to change these comparisons over and over again, for none of them can serve us for any length of time."[7] Fielding, as is evident from his own restless search for the determining image, experienced a similar difficulty as he set out to create his own uniquely innovative fiction.

I have already argued that the opening image of the novel as menu, the novelist as restaurateur, is misleading; it is, in fact, soon discarded as altogether too casual and "easy," too nonchalantly detached from the gravity of the issues to be debated. Here is one establishment where the customer is not always right, where he who pays the piper does not call the tune. It quickly becomes clear that the restaurateur is unusually adamant as to his own prerogatives; our taste buds are to be educated—if he cannot compel us to eat as he directs (to read the book as he wishes), he insists upon retaining the right to expose us as slovenly diners. At one point he goes so far as to ask us to leave the restaurant, to stop wasting our time (and his skill) on dishes too refined for our brutalized palates—those who deny the existence of love in any other than the reductionist Hobbist sense are in the wrong hotel and had better clear out (253). Fielding will not cast pearls before swine, nor set delicate viands before crude trenchermen. The management resolutely reserves the right to refuse admission.

In fact, Fielding is uneasy with the metaphor, has scarcely proposed than he revokes it, telling the reader, in a tone that brooks no
demurral, that he is in charge and intends to digress "as often as I see
occasion: of which I am myself a better judge that any pitiful critic
whatever" (54). The war against critics will continue and be extended
throughout the novel to include censurers, detractors, condemners of
all kinds, literary, moral and religious; for the moment it is enough to
note the brusque rejection of any nonsense to do with *de gustibus non
est disputandum*—the narrator, not the customer, knows best. Already
the true metaphor of judges and judgment, the one that will dominate
the novel, has intervened. The narrator denies the right of anyone to
criticize him in a form that he is pioneering; until carping critics "produce the authority by which they are constituted judges, I shall plead
to their jurisdiction," that is, question their competence (55). This
brings us to the core of the book: what makes a competent, a good
judge? This is what *Tom Jones* seeks to determine. It is a book about
courtrooms, not grillrooms, judgments, not menus; its most important
single piece of furniture is a judicial bench, not a dining table.

Yet the narrator continues to experiment with other metaphors,
ranging from government to religion. At the opening of book 2 he is
a monarch, "the founder of a new province of writing," as unchallengeable as Crusoe on his island, not "accountable to any court of
critical jurisdiction whatever" (88). He is at liberty to make his own
laws, and his erstwhile customers have now been transformed into
subjects who are bound to believe in and to obey these statutes. He is,
of course, not a *jure divino* tyrant—how could he be in a book that
condemns Thwackum as "a tyrannical rascal," declares that Western
violates nature and subverts his own authority in trying to force Sophia into an abhorrent marriage, and was written while the Jacobite
Rebellion was threatening the political settlement of 1688–89 (142,
277)? As a constitutional monarch, he is set over his subjects for their
good, not his own, created for their use, their delight and edification.
But whatever model of kingship is preferred, it is a far cry from customers at an inn. In the next book the image of the reader as subject
is replaced by a religious metaphor, when, exhorting his "young
readers" to respect and cultivate prudence, the narrator suddenly,

self-mockingly, addresses them as "my worthy disciples" (142). The range of his metaphoric search testifies to the seriousness of Fielding's concern to fix his relationship with the reader; in the images of judge and juror he found what he was seeking.

The dramatic basis of Fielding's art has long been a commonplace of criticism; the machine perfection of the plots, their Swiss clockwork precision, has often been ascribed to the fact that Fielding is the outstanding example of the dramatist turned novelist. Yet even more decisive for his art, informing every aspect of it, is the equally well-known fact that Fielding was a magistrate. The magisterial bench is our easiest access to the work; we enter his novel as though summoned to jury service, to judge action, assess character, appraise motive, scrutinize conduct, and, finally, to acquit or condemn. The obligation to be a good magistrate presses upon the reader throughout the whole of *Tom Jones*.

The narrator presides over the book like a judge over a court, always reserving the right to halt the proceedings, to intervene in order to issue a fresh set of directions or a new perspective on the evidence to the jury; to continue to call them misdirections is simply to advertise one's prejudices against Fielding's magisterial method. On the whole, as in the already cited example of our antipathy to "whores in rags," the judge's directions are unmistakable: we are being warned here to get rid of our class prejudices, to stop confusing sin and poverty, to be easier on the second or more consistently harsh on the first. Fielding is, on the whole, an intentionally less baffling interlocutor than Swift; we usually know what he means, even if we disagree with his view or find it unsatisfactory.

Take, for example, what seems like Fielding's admission that good and evil are, at bottom, mysterious and inexplicable, things given, experienced, but incapable of being captured and explained within rational formulas. Allworthy has, we learn, "a heart that hungers after goodness," but how and where he acquired this appetite, or where the reader in turn may procure it, Fielding cannot tell (58). Gide's charge that Fielding could not conceive a saint (Rawson, 341–42)—which is to say that he has no recipe, plan, or set of recommendations for the acquisition of goodness, that he cannot tell us how to *become* good—is relevant here. Tom Jones is, apparently, a hero because he is born with good impulses; when he learns some sense and acquires some maturity, this natural goodness will, so we are assured, preserve him from the indiscretions of his youth. The good man, like the good poet, is born, not made. So too, judging by Blifil, is the villain. It is, perhaps, an unexpected conclusion from the opponent of Calvinist predestination, and some readers may jib at it as unsatisfactory and evasive, provoking more questions than it answers. It is, nevertheless, the judge's direction to the jury. If there are jurors still puzzled, who want to ask, for instance, how one *becomes* a good man like Tom, how one joins the elect rather than be condemned with the reprobate Thwackums and Blifils, the court ignores the question as irrelevant, as impertinent as the misguided questions with which the foolish Partridge interrupts the Man of the Hill's tale. The direction has been given; not to comply is to be a juror who rejects competent advice. Only those who ask the right questions will receive the right answers. In a courtroom, pertinence is all.

Fielding's summons implies the confident conviction that the reader has it within him to be a good juror. Simply to be judicious is not enough; justice without generosity is no help to fallible man. Fielding presides over a court characterized by generosity, even indulgence; those condemned there will be hard pressed to find defenders anywhere. When we hear that "Thwackum was for doing justice and leaving mercy to heaven" (147), we know that he has just been categorically rejected as a candidate for Fielding's bench.

Paradoxically, Fielding distrusts jurors who are too readily or abundantly supplied with a quality that most lawyers would find desirable in those entrusted with the detection of crime: suspicion. In the final chapter, more detailed consideration will be given to the question of why Fielding should be so suspicious of suspicion. It is enough for the moment to observe that suspicion and mercy are uneasy bedfellows. Parson Adams, that naïf who "never saw farther into people than they desired to let him" (*JA*, 148), would make a very unsatisfactory magistrate; to be so consistently, unspeakably stunned at the revelation of wickedness is a disqualification in a profession that demands insight into human nature. (The affinity with Allworthy is obvious.) Yet Adams possesses a quality without which judgment verges on damnation: mercy for sinners. Told by a man, who turns out to be himself a coward, that all cowards should be hanged, Adams deplores this as far too draconian, because "men did not make themselves" (*JA*, 140). Weakness should be pitied, not punished; clemency is the way to help people overcome failings. We search Swift in vain for a comparable lenity.

True, Fielding maintains the doctrine of individual responsibility against those who would make society the scapegoat for men's sins, but his insistence is always tempered by a readiness for compassion.[8] This appeal for lenity is accompanied by a call for a reappraisal of sin, a revaluation of moral values; if it is wrong to confuse sin with poverty, it is just as misguided to identify sex with sin. Fielding tries to divert us from our Richardsonian obsession with sex; for him the really unforgivable sins are vindictiveness and heartlessness, and these are as readily found among the respectable as among the arraigned; are, indeed, all too often the occupational hazard, the industrial disease, of those who sit in judgment on their weaker brethren. Fielding the novelist treats his characters with a magistrate's expertise, using his discretionary powers to the limit, extenuating actions in the light of motives, and he clearly expects his ideal reader to do likewise. What kind of judge are you? This is the most important challenge that the reader of Fielding encounters.

The narrator involves the reader in a series of judgments, with doctrines, attitudes, and characters put on trial so that in judging them the reader judges himself. Many of these tests are sophomore exercises, virtually impossible to fail. What juror when told that Captain Blifil is "well read in Scripture," (89) will not at once see that this merely proves literacy, nothing else? Better not to know the Scriptures at all than to pervert them, as only a scholar like Blifil can, into sanctioning the punishment of illegitimate children and the prevention of charity. When virtue is the word applied to the attitude of those who condemn charity to foundlings as sinful in itself and an incitement to further sin, few readers will be puzzled as to what Fielding intends. And where is the difficulty in evaluating the narrator's observation that "the tongue of virtue . . . never fails to lash those who bring a disgrace on the sex" (60)? For Fielding, the tongue is the most unreliable of all human parts; talk is cheap and the Pharisee excels verbally, as Partridge, in danger of starving with the universal compassion of the neighbors, could wryly testify (109).

No juror will be much troubled in following Fielding's direction at moments like these. "If wenches will hang out lures for fellows"— then, presumably, they get what they deserve (71–72). So croons Bridget, telling us from a distance of two and a half centuries how we are to view actress Jodie Foster's fate in the 1988 movie *The Accused*. The accompanying aperçu that beautiful women would often have done better to have faces seamed with smallpox may sound like an echo of *The Vanity of Human Wishes,* but only the least attentive juror will be taken in. Dr. Johnson is a moralist, musing on life's ironies, among them the gifts, beauty included, that sometimes ruin their possessors: *"we witan nat what thing we preyen heere."*[9] Bridget is an ugly envious woman, disgracefully elated because her fairer sisters suffer. To miss this distinction is to exclude oneself from Fielding's jury.

There are many other instances where the test is straightforward, the burden on the potential juror as minimal as possible. The "sneerers and prophane wits" who mock Mrs. Wilkins's sexual panic at a man in his shirtsleeves are really in the right; those who, on the contrary, place any credence in her bogus apprehension would be more at home in Richardson and would be well advised to go there (56).

There is, similarly, little doubt as to where Fielding is leading us when he asks us to consider just what is, sexually, a "criminal correspondence" (76). The insistence is that we should test the moral cliché against the existential reality. Is it what Tom and Molly get up to in the thicket or is it Captain Blifil's maneuverings, his readiness to marry Allworthy's cat as soon as his sister for the sake of his money (76)? Is it the extramarital romp between Tom and Mrs. Waters at Upton or is it Lord Fellamar's resolve to make amends to Sophia through marriage after first raping her? The conventional wisdom is that marriage and sexual immorality are mutually exclusive. What, then, are we to think of Fitzpatrick's "honourable" designs (519) to get possession of a lady's fortune through marriage? Or of Blifil's nefarious scheme, reversing Fellamar's and even more noxious, to marry Sophia first and rape her afterwards, her open detestation simply giving an additional edge to his perverted appetite, an incentive to matrimony (316–17)? Yet Thwackum, so fiercely denunciatory of Tom's affair with Molly, supports Blifil's wooing of Sophia simply because the end is marriage. Legalism tyrannizes over life; society condemns Tom and congratulates Blifil. Fielding challenges conventional moral wisdom; what happened in the thicket and at Upton is not merely wholesome but almost holy compared with what Blifil means to do to Sophia with the blessing of the Church and the applause of society. Marriage, says the Pharisee, is better than fornication; that depends on the marriage, is Fielding's rejoinder, and he expects us to side with him rather than with the orthodox legalists.

The choice is just as straightforward and simple in the interchange between Sophia and Honour on the respective merits of Tom and Blifil. Honour upholds the conventional moral code that Fielding comes to subvert. She praises Blifil as a man who has no dealings with trollops and no bastards to his charge (294); she might just as easily have added that he never gets drunk. He must, therefore, be a good man. Fielding disputes not the description but the conclusion: Blifil, all that Honour claims notwithstanding, is nevertheless a rascal. The implicit challenge is to say what we mean by goodness. Fielding offers a choice between two representative men, two antithetical types: one sexually respectable and abstemious but devoid of compassion, the other compassionate but intemperate and sexually reckless; the former a man whose only love affair is with himself, the latter a man who, generously, if foolishly, spends himself with others.

Some readers, disliking these alternatives, demand a third option, a man with Tom's good nature but none of his failings, a man in whom inner worth is allied to outer decorum, a paragon. It is about as sensible as objecting to the choice between Fanny and Mary in *Mansfield Park* or Napoleon and Boxer in *Animal Farm*; indeed, the unreason is even greater in Fielding's case in view of the caution we have heard him deliver against the folly of requiring an impossible perfection here on earth. Where, within Fielding's novel—the one he wrote, not the one we might have preferred him to write—does goodness lie? With Tom or Blifil, fornicator or Pharisee? *That* is the case we are summoned to judge; it is evasive, dishonest, to shirk a decision by ignoring the problem at hand in favor of one of our own devising. If, however, we do honestly declare that we approve neither, finding, in a kind of plague-a'-both-your-houses spirit, little to choose between them, we have disqualified ourselves from serving on Fielding's jury. When Lady Mary Wortley Montagu rejects Tom as a sorry scoundrel, when Thackeray complains that he is the undeserving recipient of life's plum-cake (Rawson, 132, 279), Fielding simply invites them to leave the jury box as incompetent jurors.

Inevitably, Fielding has been associated with the alleged moral laxity of his hero, himself disowned as a responsible magistrate on the ground that he is too slack a scrutineer of human behavior. This is not merely a matter of imputed individual derelictions, as witnessed, for example, by his treatment of Mrs. Fitzpatrick, but of a whole attitude to life which is rebuked as sloven and reprehensible. (I shall argue in the final chapter that this attitude derives in fact from what Fielding regarded as the defining moral elements in Christianity.) Unquestionably, Swift would have given Mrs. Fitzpatrick short shrift as a she-Yahoo; but in Fielding's more genial view she is far from that. She does not, of course, evoke the admiration so deservedly retained for Sophia, but—sexual indiscretions notwithstanding—neither is she a worthless woman. Swift would have sent her to the Bridewell to be flayed and have her appearance changed for the worse; Christ would have countermanded the flaying, but told her to sin no more. Fielding is happy to leave her "at the polite end of town" where she "is so good an economist, that she spends three times the income of her fortune, without running into debt" (872).

The facile solution is to say that Fielding can joke about Mrs. Fitzpatrick's economic miracle because he is himself a carelessly immoral man, condoning the depravity he shares; this is the solution his rival Richardson was so quick to offer. The correct answer is that he is easy on her precisely because he *is* a moralist, a Christian moralist, though obviously of a very different school from Richardson. Fielding's target is not the sins that are seen, the gross and glaring offenses like drunkenness and fornication, but the unseen and far worse sins that sometimes fester behind fastidious facades: pride, envy, spite, malice, meanness—those prim sins that have the astonishing capacity to disguise themselves as virtues. Mrs. Fitzpatrick's sexual laxity may be balanced by her other qualities; the public scapegrace, Tom, is an immeasurably better man than the decorous Blifil. If the likes of Thwackum and Square cannot see this, so much the worse for them.

Fielding does not regard sexual promiscuity as trifling, but he refuses to accept sin and sex as synonomous; there are other, worse sins. Jenny's true seduction is financial; she is seduced by a woman for money, not by a man for pleasure. In William Kennedy's *Ironweed* the derelict heroine thanks God that she never slept with a man for money; Moll Flanders, conversely, proudly proclaims that she never slept with men for anything else. Clearly, what is involved here is not a conflict between morality and immorality, but a debate as to moral priorities and degrees of sin, a revolution in moral categories. When at the novel's close Square surprisingly crosses the courtroom to join Tom's allies as a character witness for the defense, he not only becomes a Christian, but a Christian of Fielding's persuasion, a convert to the revaluation of values proposed in the novel. Significantly, the sin that weighs most heavily on the conscience of the dying philosopher is not his furtive affair with Molly but his maligning of Tom; sexual offenses are not as serious as we think and certainly not in the same league as malice, injustice, or slander.

Fielding *is* a morally subversive writer but not in Dr. Johnson's condemnatory sense; he does not repudiate values but demands their revaluation. "How is it possible for young people to read such a book, and to look upon orderliness, sobriety, obedience, and frugality as *virtues*?" asks William Cobbett (Rawson, 400). But Cobbett's complaint about *Tom Jones* misses the point. Young people are forever being exhorted not only to regard these as virtues, but, too often, as the crucial, indeed the only, virtues. Fielding never denies that they are virtues; he simply reiterates, in his own idiom and for his own times, the key lesson of Paul's letter to the Corinthians: the insistence that without charity all these are dross. Minos at the entrance to Elysium utters the same warning: "No man enters this gate without charity."[10] Being an artist, Fielding renders the Pauline message in his own dramatically rhetorical way, but who will say that the message was, or is, redundant? The mean and spiteful do well to fear arraignment in Fielding's court; in almost every other case, he is happy to utter a *nolle prosequi.*

Like Christ challenging the Pharisees, Fielding is at once more lenient and forgiving, yet harsher and more accusing. We are told that Nightingale is scrupulously honest in the ordinary transactions of life, but a selfish cheat in affairs of love; had he used in trade or business the stratagems of deception he employs against women "he would have been counted the greatest villain upon earth" (669). Anything goes in the commerce of passion. It is Fielding's variant on the adage about patriotism: if we did for ourselves what we do for our countries, what scoundrels we should be. If we acted toward men in business as we do toward women in love, we would end up in prison. Yet society condemns the one kind of misconduct while condoning the other, turning, for once, in its arbitrarily selective way, a blind eye to sexual wrongdoing. It is not Fielding whom an honest juror will find lax or inconsistent.

At the same time, we can see that the problems being set for our solution are becoming more complex, more ticklish and taxing. How, for example, are we to assess Tom's behavior in London as he comes straight from Lady Bellaston's bed with the money that will save the would-be highwayman's family from starvation? The gigolo as savior: here is a moral conundrum to tax the ingenuity of the most engaged and intelligent juror. We despise gigolos, admire saviors; how, asks Fielding, will you react when the one is the other, when the two roles are fused? As before, in the choice between Tom and Blifil, we have to take the world as it is, not as we would like it to be. The fact that we may prefer our saviors to be sexually chaste is irrelevant in the case under consideration: Here *is* the savior—how do you like him? And lest the problem should be too simple, Fielding intensifies its intractability: Tom is not a savior who happens to be a gigolo; he is a savior *because* he is a gigolo. But for the money earned from servicing Lady Bellaston, the Anderson family would have starved to death. The reader-juror is put on the spot: Which would he prefer—a pure hero and a dead family, or a gigolo who keeps people alive? Jury service is not as simple or straightforward as we imagined.

Following the sophomore simplicity of the opening tests—seeing through Mrs. Wilkins, exposing Square—these later problems increase in complexity and difficulty. We confront Tom's ambivalent situation as kept man and savior combined; we are made to consider the problematic status and value of prudence as an element in the moral life, the ticklish question as to whether we should shun or foster suspicion as a quality of human nature. The solution of the twin problems of prudence and suspicion are best left until we consider the peculiar blend of Christianity and comedy wherein Fielding chose to present his artistic vision of life. What can now profitably be discussed is the problem of Allworthy—his persistent failure throughout the novel to see through trickery, to discriminate between cheats and truth tellers, which results in his habitual vulnerability to deception. Profitably, because in appraising Fielding's defense of Allworthy against the charge of gullibility, we shall simultaneously reveal certain essential elements of Fielding's art, notably his strategy for discomfiting the pharisaical reader. A writer so hard on the Pharisee as character was not likely to go easy on the Pharisee as reader.

Allworthy has always seemed one of the puzzles of the book. As early as 1792 James Henry Pye condemned him as "the dupe of every insinuating rascal he meets; and a dupe not of the most amiable kind, since he is always led to acts of justice and severity. The consequence of his pliability is more often the punishment of the innocent than the acquittal of the guilty; and in such punishment he is severe and implacable" (Rawson, 190–91). Admittedly, Allworthy's persistent mistakes reasonably lead one to conclude that, despite his benevolence, he is a fool, a well-meaning dupe who is too easily taken in. And yet, invariably accompanying each mistake, is the narrator's insistent warning to the reader not to be censorious: Allworthy is no fool and we are strictly forbidden to think so. The troublesome question nevertheless remains: how can this good and sensible man go on being so consistently wrong?

The Christian, striving to reconcile God's goodness with his omnipotence, knows a similar embarrassment: How can God be at once all-powerful and all-good? Either he can but will not stop evil (we save the omnipotence by sacrificing the goodness); or he wishes to stop evil but cannot (the goodness is saved at the cost of the power). In *Tom Jones* the narrator faces a similar quandary: How is he to maintain at the same time Allworthy's benevolence and his judgment? The judgment, clearly, is most at risk. If the good man cannot see that the tutors are bad, as the reader so easily does, then his vision must surely be defective. Yet the narrator assures us that Allworthy "had much discernment" in recognizing and supporting men of genius and learning (74); there seems no good reason for regarding this as sarcasm, and in any case the narrator goes on defending, sometimes testily, Allworthy against the charge of gullibility to the novel's end. In the culminating reconciliation between the newly enlightened parent and the wronged son, so cruelly miscast as prodigal in the unjust exile from Paradise Hall, Tom refuses to blame Allworthy in the slightest for the errors that have caused such distress (Allworthy, as has been noted, tempers his own self-recrimination by attaching some of the responsibility to Tom's imprudence): "The wisest man might be deceived as you were" (853). It is the narrator's recurring defense of Allworthy, reinforced by issuing from the mouth of the man who has best cause to rebuke the blunders, to fault the faulty judgment. If Tom, supported by the narrator, finds no case against Allworthy, why should the reader complain? If Isabella wishes to forgive Angelo, why should Coleridge be so indignant? Whose business is it, anyway?

The narrator, however, is unwilling that it should simply be a matter of the reader's gratuitous forbearance; behind *Tom Jones,* as behind *Measure for Measure,* is the Christian ethic, the idea that forgiveness is not just something we give out of the goodness of our hearts, but out of the necessity of our souls: we give what we need. We are to forgive Allworthy (Tom and reader alike) for the most urgent of reasons—he is a man like ourselves, frail and fallible, and if he makes mistakes, that simply identifies a fellow sinner. As Fielding reminds us, there are no gods or superhuman beings in his book, no infallible paragons, only men and women, and the spoor of the human is error (137). If Allworthy fails, his failure reflects no credit on us; on the contrary, the aim is to chasten us, to remind us of what we have in common—there but for the grace of Fielding go I. This Christian insight becomes one of the informing principles, the armature, the structural pillar, of Fielding's narrative style.

The reader quite naturally sees that it might well be politic for Tom to forgive, since he himself stands in such need of forgiving; Sophia has much to overlook before Tom achieves his felicity. But, just as naturally, the reader is not conscious of any defect in himself, at least as *reader,* that puts him in the same vulnerable predicament as the wayward hero. The reader takes his place within the book like the Pharisee in the temple, sensibly and justly aware of his own superiority to a fornicator like Tom and a fool like Allworthy: I thank thee, God, that I am not like other men. At this point, like Christ before him, Fielding launches his attack. Not simply content to beg the reader's indulgence for the blunderer, the narrator goes on the offensive, insisting that because Allworthy does not see what is so plain to the reader does not necessarily make him a fool or in any sense culpable: Allworthy is not blameworthy. As Fielding shockingly turns on the reader, challenging him to ponder the source of his own superior insight, the origin and roots of his greater perceptiveness, the stage is set for a contest between narrator and reader. What makes Allworthy so unseeing and the reader so hawkeyed? The reader can tell us: Allworthy is a fool whereas he is clever. Fielding has a very different explanation, and, in advancing it, he mortifyingly uncovers certain truths about art in general and his own fiction in particular.

His rebuke to the reader is simple to the point of banality: if the reader sees and knows more than Allworthy, that is simply because he *is* a reader while Allworthy is a character, an actor. Allworthy finds himself thrown into a fiction (*he* does not know this) as we, in Heidegger's term *Geworfenheit,* find ourselves thrown into life (is that too a fiction?). He meets other characters as we meet other people, becomes existentially enmeshed in situations, where, without the aid of a text, he has to assess and judge, react and initiate. We, in life, know only too well how difficult this is, how prone to error we are. Life is not a text, a story shaped and ordered for us by a narrator; life offers no standing invitation to us to pause, reflect, backtrack, recall, reconsider, revise, laying it aside when we feel fatigued, returning to it when we are refreshed, more inspired. Above all, we cannot assume in life, as until recently we could with a text, that all is coherent, meaningful, patterned, interrelated; art is form, life formlessness. All art is a reflection and an imitation of that first great original act of creation and every artist is a second maker, a rival God, whether in enmity or reverence.

Allworthy exists, without knowing it, in a work of art; *he* confronts the dissemblers with no narrative shield reassuringly between him and them. The reader, by contrast, continually sees the cheats through the medium of the narrator's ironic, qualifying language; they are made of words for us, but not for Allworthy. It is one of the triumphs of Fielding's art to make us forget this, which necessarily entails making us simultaneously forget how dependent we are on him. There is here an important anticipation of television. Television is based on the supposition that seeing is believing, when the reality of television is that seeing is deceiving. We are fooled into accepting the screen as a window, transparent, through which we survey the real world, when in truth the screen is an opaque surface on which various artificial images are projected. We delude ourselves that we are looking *through* when we are looking *at*; we watch a fabrication, something imposed on the real world, not, as we imagine, the real world itself. Fielding, similarly, creates the reality we look at; if we know Blifil so well, it is because he has been so completely created for us. But, it must be repeated, he has not been thus created for Allworthy; his Blifil is not the reader's. Remembering this, we will not be censorious; failing to do so, we will be chasteningly reminded.

How is Allworthy to share in the reader's insight, to *see,* for instance, that Thwackum's meditations are full of birch (133)? How can we, in life, make windows into men's souls? And we must never forget that what is art for us is "life" for Allworthy. Even in the nightmarish Oceania of Orwell's *Nineteen Eighty-four* Winston Smith smiles (at least to begin with) at the arrogance of O'Brien's claim to be able to unpack the contents of another person's skull. The reader of *Tom Jones* needs no such unbelievable penetrative power, for the narrator enters skulls and souls on his behalf; the reader is *told* that Thwackum forever dreams of flogging. But Allworthy is not. The reader knows, not because he is more clever, but because he is more privileged, more informed. It is not a difference between intelligence and stupidity, but between a man reading and a man living, for when we read we are always more godlike than when we live.

Because the reader is privileged, he must not be proud; once again the Christian infrastructure is visible. The reader must constantly recall that the gift he has received is precisely that: a gift, an endowment, not a proof of personal achievement or a cause for self-esteem. "The reader is greatly mistaken, if he conceives that Thwackum appeared to Mr. Allworthy in the same light as he doth to him in this history" (136). The reader's Thwackum and Allworthy's Thwackum are two different men. Hence the naïveté of the reader's error when he wonders how Allworthy could have missed what is so obvious to him: Thwackum is so patently a bad man that Allworthy must be very foolish not to have seen it. This is precisely the foolish arrogance that Fielding attacks; the reader "is as much deceived, if he imagines, that the most intimate acquaintance which he himself could have had with that divine, would have informed him of those things which we, from our inspiration, are enabled to open and discover" (136). Life and art are separate, discontinuous realms, requiring disparate modes of apprehending. It is folly or, worse still, conceit to claim that we would have seen through Thwackum even without the narrator's help; it is moreover absurd because without the narrator there would be no Thwackum to see through. If what is really meant is that we would never be taken in by a Thwackum in real life, this is mere bombast, based on the silly assumption that Thwackum in life would be the same pellucid, easily judged character that he is in art. And even art, as Fielding will so chasteningly, mortifyingly show, has its deceptions; in art David failed to know himself, far less another human being, and Nathan stunned the indignant king into ashamed silence by pointing out that *he* was the man.

We recall (and are meant to recall) that the Pharisee's chief impertinence was to credit to himself what was due to God, to claim as merit what was really grace. It is just as impertinent and ungrateful when the reader condemns Allworthy for not knowing what would have escaped him, too, but for the narrator's art, to reproach Allworthy for lacking the grace so freely given to himself. We are to be thankful for the privileged information, not merciless to those from whom it has been withheld. "Of readers who from such conceits as these, condemn the wisdom or penetration of Mr. Allworthy, I shall not scruple to say, that they make a very bad and ungrateful use of that knowledge which we have communicated to them" (136–37). The author-God rebukes the Pharisee reader. At the opening of book 10, the narrator, adopting the tone if not the idiom of God rebuking Job, warns the little reptile-critic not to be too hastily presumptuous in attempting to judge the great creation of the book, when so much of it inevitably lies hidden to his view (467). It would be a mistake to see only the humor here and miss the even more important underlying seriousness. The author-God will not abide man's arrogance, whether it be, as with the reptile-critic, the arrogance of ignorance, or, as with the censurer of Allworthy, the arrogance of knowledge, especially when that knowledge is a narrative gift and not the harvest of merit. Is everyone *in* the play a dolt because we see through "honest" Iago and they do not? Do we lack the humility to admit that we are beholden to Shakespeare's art, not to our own presumed superior insight?

There is an echo here of Swift denouncing those moderns who claimed superiority to the ancients by virtue of their possession of the truths of Christianity; unable to deny the claim, Swift chooses to deride it instead. The egregious modern of the *Tale of a Tub* clinches his indictment of Homer by exposing his gross ignorance of the doctrine and discipline of the Anglican Church in a *reductio ad absurdum* of the idiocy of blaming the ancients for having been born before, and praising ourselves for having been born after, the Incarnation.[11] The young clergyman is warned against the insufferable cant of disparaging the ancient philosophers whose fault is "that they were ignorant of certain facts which happened long after their death."[12] If we are Christians, we owe it solely to a gratuitous revelation;[13] if the ancient philosophers never achieved a satisfactory idea of God, what more can be expected of reason without revelation? The God who mercifully reveals himself would otherwise be a *deus absconditus*; how blasphemous to claim credit when, bereft of the revelation, we should be as sunk in ignorance as ever the ancients were. Swift is resolved not to allow his fellow Christians to flaunt their gift of religion as proof of superiority to those who lived before Christ.

It is the mark of the Pharisee to pride himself on his superiority. Fielding is attacking any tendency to Pharisaism in the reader. Allworthy *is* a fool, consistently deluded; it is tempting to dismiss him as such and rest easy in our own superior sagacity. Yet again, the Christian framework is vital to an understanding of Fielding's art. The adulterous woman *was* a sinner and did, legally, deserve stoning. Jesus disputed neither point, but simply invited the sinless ones to throw the first stones. Fielding, similarly, defies the reader to condemn Allworthy, insisting that, but for his assistance, the reader would have been equally mistaken—an argument impossible to refute, because we depend entirely on the narrator for all we know of Thwackum. Allworthy's mistakes should remind us of our own fallibility; they are not meant to be a matter of self-congratulation.

Consider, for example, what, in terms of its repercussions, must be seen as the greatest single instance of human gullibility in literature or legend: the error of Eve that led to the loss of Eden. Milton in *Paradise Lost* refers to "our credulous mother,"[14] and there is, undeniably, a criticism in the adjective. Naturally, this is so. It is not good for anyone to be credulous. It was not good for Eve to be so. She should have been more vigilant, less trusting—this is the unmistakable implication.

But it would be the grossest of misreadings to take Milton as meaning that we were somehow unfortunate in our foolish first mother, that another conceivable first mother might have served us better. Eve is not being singled out for special, unique condemnation in the sense that, but for her, this individual woman with her own peculiar credulity, we, her children, would still be in paradise. Milton is no more saying that than Orwell is saying that mankind was just unlucky in having a weakling like Winston as our last champion. In both cases, Eden and Oceania alike, the fall would have occurred, whoever our representative: any first mother, given the same set of circumstances, would have been as credulous as Eve; any last champion, subjected to the same pressures, will capitulate like Winston. That, at least, is surely what Milton and Orwell intend; the faults of their protagonists are those of humanity, the reader included. Similarly circumstanced, the reader, too, would have been credulous or fearful; to deny this is mere braggadocio. Likewise in Fielding: if Allworthy blunders, it is because men, readers included, are blunderers all.

It is so tempting for readers, like Pharisees or Christians, to turn privilege and grace into personal merit, instruments of superiority. Readers can be Pharisees too; and, having flayed them as characters *in* the text, Fielding is in no mood for lenity when he finds them as readers *of* it.

Hence Fielding's unceasing battle to protect Allworthy from the reader's censure. Allworthy, we are told, was not blind to faults in Thwackum—though he failed to spot the flagrant ones revealed to us, courtesy of the narrator—but hoped rather that they might be balanced or nullified by the opposing faults he detected in Square. Yet even Fielding, partisan as he is for Allworthy, cannot finally argue that things worked out according to Allworthy's plan; far from canceling each other, the bad tutors, despite their ideological enmity, conspire together against Tom. Nevertheless, here, too, Fielding has an unanswerable argument. Allworthy has, it must be admitted, made a mistake; has the reader never made one? "If the event happened contrary to his expectations, this possibly proceeded from some fault in the plan itself; which the reader hath my leave to discover if he can: for we do not pretend to introduce any infallible characters into this history; where we hope nothing will be found which hath never yet been seen in human nature" (137). To err is human. Since there are no infallible judges in real life, why should there be in an art that simulates real life, rejecting romance in favor of history?

Fielding can the more confidently challenge the reader because he knows that at bottom the reader is just as fallible as Allworthy, not merely in life but within the pages of *Tom Jones* itself. *Tom Jones* is a text deliberately and meticulously crafted to frustrate the Pharisaism of the reader, to show him that he is finally just as gullible, as easily misled, as convinced that he is in the right when he is completely wrong, as any blundering character within the book. Just as there are no infallible characters in the text, so there are no infallible readers of the text, at least first time round—Fielding sees to that. The text must be read twice to be grasped once; its aim is to teach, not just Tom, but the reader to know himself, and the self that emerges from this tuition is fallible, leaping to hasty conclusions, swallowing unproved assumptions, going completely astray at certain nodal points of the action: a self that is twin to Allworthy's. Even while the reader censures Allworthy, he is committing the same faults, as Fielding fully intends. We are drawn, without our consent, without even our awareness, into a chastening comedy to swell the prologue of the gullible and deceived. How, we ask ourselves in retrospect, were we so easily fooled? How did we stray so far from truth?—the same questions that Allworthy puts to himself. And he has more excuse than we do, because *he* was not taken into Tom's heart to be shown how sound and decent it was, appearances notwithstanding. Confession of sin is the first step toward virtue. The reader is shown the second time around that he was a bad reader and a bad judge, not so that he will never go wrong again (an impossible ambition), but so that he may learn the humility and forbearance without which every reader, every judge, is a Pharisee.

The first-time reader admires the life, the vitality, of the novel, but at the expense of its art; it is the gusto of the performance that impresses the reader who is still not privy to the total design. Too many critics were for too long content to praise Fielding along such lines, hence the development of a certain patronizing view of Fielding as a great primitive, coarse, racy, a good storyteller, important as a historical marker in the development of the novel, but cruelly limited when set against such masters as Jane Austen, Dickens, or George Eliot. One is tempted to say that such critics are the one-time readers of *Tom Jones,* for it is only on a second reading, when all is now known (in spite of certain highly sophisticated modern readings of *Tom Jones,* the fact remains that we cannot *unknow*),[15] that the subtlety of the art can be fully appreciated. It follows that the second reading is a chastening rebuke to the first, a deliberate humiliation of its brash confidence, an exercise in modest self-knowledge. What we *knew* turns out to be only what we thought we knew; we knew we were right and are shown to be wrong. Fielding's liberal lesson is plain: knowledge, however rock-solid it seems, may be built on sand; what can happen in *Tom Jones* can the more easily happen in life. Judge not lest ye be judged. But if, as necessity dictates, you have to judge, then do so reluctantly, provisionally, and, above all, generously.

On a second reading the abashed reader becomes the observer of his own mistakes and of the deceptively good reasons he had for making them. Fielding's underlying aim is not to excuse these past mistakes, nor even, in a sense, to prevent future ones—rather it is to instill and encourage in the reader a certain attitude of mind, a disposition toward life, which, though not making him infallible, will make him more forgiving. For what we forgive in ourselves, we shall surely not fault in others. Empson talks of the reader being teased (Rawson, 528), but that is too weak a term. Behind Fielding's gulling of the reader is more than just a sense of fun, a humorist's delight in play; the aim is far more serious than that. The reader is being tested, not teased, tried and found wanting, not for the purpose of condemning him but to dissuade him from condemning others.

The reader who continues, despite the narrator's warnings, to blame Allworthy for being taken in has, ironically, without knowing it, suffered the same fate. If Allworthy is a fool, what is he? He sees through Thwackum with ease, but is blinded by Bridget. Why, if he is so sharp at detecting frauds, is the perspicacity so selective, so limited?

Why does it operate so infallibly in some cases while collapsing in others? The honest answer is that we rely upon the narrator, and the narrator is not always reliable. In the matter of Tom's parentage, for example, the narrator acts toward the reader as Blifil does toward Allworthy—deceiving and dissembling—and the reader is just as hoodwinked, as helpless, as Allworthy. The narrator has been secretly laughing at his simpleton reader much as Dr. Blifil sniggers at the sermonizing Allworthy (84), and laughing the more because the simpleton is so proud of his penetration, his alert disinclination to be led astray. When pots call kettles black, the man who keeps the kitchen may well smile.

The narrator opens with an invitation to the reader to join him as companion; the invisible observer has heard Bridget's bell ring for breakfast and invites us to answer the summons with him—"where I must attend, and, if you please, shall be glad of your company" (59). What could be more sociable, more friendly? We have fallen in with a good companion who generously extends to us the privilege of his own invisibility—a place at the breakfast table, not, of course, to eat, but to listen, to watch, and, friendlier still, to have the action halted so that our knowing companion can explain, observe, comment, and, in general, keep us informed. The implicit but unmistakable promise is that we are in good narrative hands, sharing in all that he knows. Only the second time around do we realize that the pose of compatriot is a deception, that we have fallen into the hands of a false friend who knows much more than he tells, and worse still, who deliberately and systematically leads us astray while pretending an ignorance from which he is really free.

He annotates Allworthy's remark to Bridget about having a present for her: "for which she thanked him, imagining, I suppose, it had been a gown" (59). Why should we disbelieve so innocent a speculation from our new friend concerning Bridget's reaction to her brother's words? Yet all the time the narrator knows that Bridget is the foundling's mother and that *she* knows what the present truly is. The deception is sustained: "But if such was her expectation . . ."; he knows that a gown is *not* her expectation, that what she expects to hear is news of the baby whom she and Jenny have conspired to place in Allworthy's bed. When Mrs. Wilkins brings in the child, Bridget is silent—a silence the narrator dishonestly attributes to her great surprise, when he knows that she is not at all surprised, that things are working out exactly as she planned. And what, in retrospect, could be more deceptive than the following? "Her brother . . . told her the whole story, which, as the reader knows already, we shall not repeat" (59). What a piece of impertinence this is on a second reading—how sweetly we are taken in. How can Allworthy tell what he does not know? Allworthy and the reader are linked in a delusion of knowing the whole story when it is Bridget and the narrator who really know it while pretending not to; Bridget is to her brother what the narrator is to the reader: a dissembler, a cheat. Not till the book's end will Allworthy and the reader know the whole story; meanwhile the narrator colludes with Bridget to keep it from us.

Mrs. Wilkins (who can be presumed to know her mistress) confidently expects her to spurn the child in loathing, but, instead, Bridget remarkably, unpredictably, takes "the good natur'd" side of the question along with her benevolent brother (60). In what is presented as a contrary-to-fact conditional, we are told that Bridget's instructions for the infant's care could not have been more solicitous "had it been a child of her own" (61). The narrator proceeds to speculate as to the reasons for this, all the while mockingly aware that he has just told us the real reason, but in such a way that we are bound to miss it. When Bridget launches into a tirade of abuse against the child's mother, employing every epithet in the calendar of female infamy, the smoke-screen is intensified. On a first reading this is easily, naturally seen as the punitive indignation of the unforgiving Pharisee, the stoner of adulteresses—which Bridget so plainly is. Only a second reading reveals the ironic truth: that Bridget stages a show of stunning hypocrisy in order to divert any hint of suspicion from herself; the outraged moralist is the fallen woman. In both readings she says what we expect, but the motive is very different. There is, of course, no mystery about Bridget's motive for deception; more intriguing is why the narrator should be so obliging in preserving her secret.

To answer "for the sake of the suspense" is true but trite. Of course the mystery of Tom's parentage must be withheld from us as from Allworthy, so that the final revelation may be at once a triumphant surprise and a longed-for liberation. But if *Tom Jones* is the masterpiece of achieved art, the consummate fusion of form and content, the one reinforcing the other, that is the argument of this study, then it must be more than a mere matter of melodramatic suspense, of delayed recognition, however delightfully and precisely crafted this should be. Nor is it simply a leg-pull, the great humorist playing tricks on his reader, enjoying himself hugely at the gull's expense, undeniably present though this element, too, is in the work. The fooling of the reader is an integral, indispensable part of the novel, a function of its meaning; in a book about love and judgment, the reader is being warned to judge lovingly, "for the measure you give will be the measure you get back." Go easy on Allworthy; you are no infallible paragon yourself. If you want forgiveness, learn to forgive. The narrative style, the form created by Fielding for his fable, matches perfectly its moral meaning, supplementing and strengthening the entire structure in a reciprocity of significance.

It is the foolish, the dangerous judge who thinks that judgment is easy. If it were so, neither reader nor Allworthy would ever be taken in. Fielding's novel is shaped to stress the difficulty of judgment; there is, indeed, a suppressed yet discernible nostalgia for a world in which judgment would be obsolete, anachronistic, unnecessary. The magistrate who must judge is most aware of the fallibility of courts. (We shall consider in the concluding chapter how decisive is this nostalgia in creating the Christian comedy so strikingly unique to Fielding). Jenny at the outset presents a piquant instance of this difficulty. We expect courts to contain guilty people pretending to be blameless and so we train ourselves to detect the infamy that hides behind a surface innocence; but what judicial procedure will enable us to see through innocence pretending to be guilt? Jenny, in a sense, *has* been seduced, has parted with her honor, not for passion, but for coin; but who among us would have rejected the confession that Allworthy so naturally believes?

The narrator's compliment (ironic in retrospect) to "the sagacious reader" (71) is offered in the knowledge that the reader has gone completely astray; the very clues planted concerning Bridget's motherhood are supplied in the gleeful assurance that the reader will miss them. The retrospective relish with which the narrator tells us that Mrs. Wilkins has been "steering a wrong course" is obvious, for the reader, unlike the housekeeper, continues to steer a wrong course with the "help" of an untrustworthy navigator-narrator (71). Nor will it do for the reader who censoriously condemns Allworthy to complain in turn that the narrator has deceived him; Blifil deceived Allworthy. We can scarcely cry foul in the one case and not in the other. Simpler, more honest, more moral to admit the truth: judgment is not easy, either for us or for Allworthy.

In any case, Allworthy's foolishness is sometimes of that almost commendable kind (certainly for Fielding) that marks the moral innocent, the person laudably unacquainted with evil. Swift knows this type, too, as his fool among knaves alternative reveals: the sense in which the Giant King is a fool for rejecting the secret of gunpowder, or the Houyhnhnm Master bewildered by the depravities that we so incriminatingly comprehend, or Gulliver himself for failing to readapt to the Yahoo life to which he has returned. These are fools only because their adversaries are knaves. Allworthy talks sense and virtue, but he talks it to rogues and liars who laugh at him behind his back. He exhorts Jenny to repent a fall that has never occurred; he condemns the profanation of marriage in general while blessing his sister's particular desecration (68, 83–84). The irony is, of course, at his expense too; where is the good of a knowledge so ineptly applied, of a perfect theory and a witless practice? Sermons to such as Dr. Blifil are a waste of breath—but, it must be repeated, we know this only because we were told.

Lest we become too puffed up with our own perspicacity, we are sometimes brought up against the blank wall of the narrator's own ignorance. Why *did* Jenny jump up from her chair and smile and blush? "I know not for what reason," says the narrator (92), leaving us to ask, "Who does, then?" In life we observe acts, not motives; we see, at best, what happens, the external event, but not why it happens, the internal impulse. Mrs. Partridge sees Jenny's actions and interprets them as proof of adultery. But the best of us are only eyewitnesses and the evidence is almost always circumstantial, always Janus-faced: "perhaps . . . possibly . . . whether . . . or." Because we cannot know for sure, the safest course is not to leap with Mrs. Partridge toward conclusions or kitchen knives, but to be humble and patient toward data, postponing judgment for as long as we can.

Conversely, when we *do* know, when through art we have been taken into the few cubic centimeters of the skull, acquiring an intimacy we could never possess in life, we should acknowledge our debt to the narrator and not condemn Allworthy for lacking our privilege. Mrs. Partridge tells the neighbors that her husband is a wife-beating adulterer; we, unlike them, know this is untrue. But they, too, would know if they were reading *Tom Jones* instead of being in it. Mrs. Partridge swears to Allworthy that she caught her husband and Jenny in bed together; we know that she is perjuring herself—Allworthy does not (98). Is it reasonable to fault him for failing to see through such irrational self-ruinous rage? We are at the mercy of such madness, the more so when it comes to us not as fury but as cool common sense. In the inn at Gloucester a lawyer, deliberately, with pure, disinterested malice, tells the landlady a pack of lies about Tom, and when she, originally prejudiced in Tom's favor by his frank, handsome appearance, hints her disbelief, the liar swears to the truth of his indictment, impudently appealing for verification to what is most outrageous in his slanders: "What interest have I in taking away the reputation of a man who never injured me?" (390). But, as Melville asks, how much money did the devil make by gulling Eve?[16] The lawyer's "reason" for maligning Tom is simply the unreason of malice. Othello is spokesman for the anguished bewilderment of those on the receiving end of such monstrously irrational injustice:

> Will you, I pray, demand that
> demi-devil
> Why he hath thus ensnared
> my soul and body?[17]

The trouble is the plausibility, the convincing-ness, of such irrational-ism: the lawyer must be telling the truth, for there is no other rational explanation. However reluctantly, the deceived landlady is forced to believe the slanders: "she looked on our heroe as a sorry scoundrel, and therefore treated him as such, for which not even Jones himself, had he known as much as the reader, could have blamed her" (391). Once again, it is only the reader's privileged position that saves him from the landlady's error. Fielding rebukes those readers too conceited to admit this: if we are "saved," it is because we have been saved, not because we have saved ourselves.

It is interesting to contrast Fielding with Cervantes on this point. In *Don Quixote* Cervantes is concerned to abolish or at least blur the boundaries between art and life, suggesting that our assumptions as to the fabrications of the one and the stability of the other are less firmly grounded than we suppose.[18] The world, too, is a fiction in which we act, assuming roles, performing parts. As characters within this fiction we are not privileged, but stand in the same relation to life as Allworthy does to the plot of *Tom Jones,* and are just as liable to error and confusion, to the seductive sway of appearances. Kundera hails Cervantes as the great hero of the novel for being the first to discover its true wisdom, the wisdom of uncertainty. We cannot know; the greatness of the novel as genre depends on its epistemological hu-mility, its courage in confronting the inescapable human condition: the impossibility of cognitive finality.[19]

In the final chapter I shall argue that Fielding's comic art, on the contrary, depends entirely for its acceptance on just such an assurance of cognitive finality, a conviction that, as the Gospel promises, all things will be revealed in time, no mysteries left unexplained, no de-serts unrewarded, no villainies unpunished—at the Last Judgment, the *parousia,* the whole world and its history will be made known, laid bare. It is this cognitive confidence, this epistemological aplomb, that underwrites the happy endings, ratifies the final rescues, of Fielding's art. If he is the great comedian, it is because for him, as a matter of faith, life is ultimately comic, a revelation and a resolution. Fielding's art reprieves us from the uncertainties, confusions, and ambiguities of life. His work, in sharp contrast to the Spaniard's, sets us securely above the painful provisionality of life. However manifold the misunderstandings, they are only temporary and will be resolved. The reader knows from the outset that Tom is good, Blifil bad, as he could never so surely know in life, and at the end Allworthy and all the other characters will share in this cognitive certainty.

Nevertheless, as has been noted, Fielding as artist resents the reader's smug assumption that his knowledge is self-inspired, the fruit of his own insight. It is so insidiously easy to be a Pharisee-reader, because, inevitably, the onlooker sees more than the participant, the spectator more than the player. We arrogantly presume that we would not be deluded like the simpletons we survey: Eve, Brutus, Othello, Isabel Archer, Billy Budd, Gatsby, every one an innocent, a dupe, deficient in the acuity we so abundantly possess. Fielding's literary strategy is to strike at the roots of this arrogance. To this end, in addition to the irony that is directed at his Pharisee-characters, he recruits a second type, subversive, discomforting, for use against his Pharisee-readers.

This irony requires a most remarkable self-discipline, a controlled reticence, a self-denying ordinance, on the part of the author. He must, with heroic discretion, conceal some of his most consummate ironies, hiding rather than highlighting his own skills. Such ironies must patiently await a second reading before their impact can be felt and before the complacent reader realizes for the first time how thoroughly he has been misled. It is as if Fielding, having told us so much, only to hear us churlishly claim all the credit of our knowing for ourselves, suddenly decided, without warning, to withhold information, planting true clues that we are sure to miss and false clues that we are sure to follow, in what seems suspiciously like a retaliation. Fielding challenges the Pharisee-reader: if he is as clever as he claims, if he insists on misconstruing the narrator's grace as his own merit, then let us see what happens when grace is denied and he is left to his own resources. Suppose the narrator ceases to be the obliging informant and becomes instead a withholder, or worse still, a distorter, of information; suppose the narrator becomes a Blifil for the reader—how will the reader fare then? The quarrel between Tom and Blifil following Allworthy's recovery will show us just how vulnerable, how dependent, the reader is.

The second-time reader is conscious that the opening books of the novel are laden with ironies stemming from the fact that Tom is Bridget's firstborn son, Blifil's elder brother, Allworthy's rightful heir. The plot that evoked Coleridge's unstinted praise owes its excellence to Fielding's superb contrivance in simultaneously supplying the clues to, yet postponing the discovery of, Tom's parentage until the appropriately artistic moment. Yet the eulogistic comparison with *Oedipus Rex* and *The Alchemist* is, if anything, unfair to Fielding. Unlike these dramatic works. *Tom Jones* is a long and complex novel that no reader could assimilate at one sitting or hold in his mind as a coherent whole. Not only can these ironies not be appreciated at a first reading, not only are they prodigally thrown away upon a first-time reader; so many, so detailed are they that they cannot be fully remembered at the novel's end—here is the difference from Sophocles or Jonson—but can only be savored by someone rereading the book. To read *Tom Jones* once is to misread it, to miss its essential greatness; unless we read twice, we have, in a crucial sense, not read at all.

Only on a second reading can we appreciate the dramatically ironic import of the quarrel between Tom and Blifil at Allworthy's sickbed. The first reading tells us that Bridget is dead—the truth, but not the whole truth. Just as stunning as Blifil's deception of Tom is the narrator's deception of the reader. Fielding joins with the villain in suppressing Bridget's dying words revealing the secret of Tom's birth. Only the second reading reveals the implications of this discovery. What at first seemed simply a quarrel between two men who dislike each other is shown to be yet another instance of that immemorial fratricidal strife that dates from Cain and Abel. That this Abel does not even know his adversary makes it the more ironic. Cain knows, as does the narrator. The novel is a different novel the second time round. On a first reading, Blifil, however ungracious and resentful, has a certain justification; Tom's drunken joy sits ill with Blifil's grief for his newly dead mother, as the contrite Tom himself generously concedes. It *is* wrong for Tom to be rioting while Blifil grieves. We like

Tom, but sympathize with Blifil. On a second reading Blifil's behavior is seen as unpardonable, monstrous, the most impudent piece of villainy in the novel. For Blifil now knows that *his* mother, the dead woman, is also Tom's mother. Yet he can still utter the taunt about illegitimacy, mockingly congratulating his unknowing brother on his good fortune, in that he cannot mourn the death of parents whom he does not know. It is cruel, unforgivable. Tom would mourn his dead mother, were Blifil decent enough to reveal Dowling's news. Blifil has the gall to rebuke Tom for not doing what he himself prevents. It is the nadir of nastiness in the book, but it is lost on the first-time reader. So much is Fielding prepared to risk in order to make his attack upon the Pharisee-reader. Those who do not reread have missed it for ever.

It is a cliché of criticism that *Tom Jones* must be read twice before it can be properly understood; far from being a new insight, this is the almost instinctive reaction of any student of the book. What has not been sufficiently interrogated is Fielding's rationale for choosing to tell his story in this way. Why does he conceal his own cleverness, run the risk that the splendid ironies may be lost or neglected, deny his own merits to the first inspection, almost as if he were following the parable advice as to how to behave when attending a wedding feast? It is certainly true that any reappraisal of *Tom Jones* will lead to the work being told, like the self-effacing guest, to go higher. There is small cause for any modern reader, who gives to Fielding the critical attention he deserves, to condescend to *Tom Jones* as a pioneering work in the limiting sense of that adjective—early, therefore crude. There is sophistication and subtlety here to test any reader, despite the strictures of Leavis, Kermode, and others. If behind every art, at however distant a remove, is a metaphysic, a way of understanding life, then we should look to St. Paul's letter to the Corinthians to find the vision that informs and sustains *Tom Jones*. Not simply, important though it is, to the passage exalting charity above all other things in heaven or on earth, the passage that supplied Fielding with the armory for his war against the unforgiving Pharisees, characters and readers alike: do not rush to judgment; you may be mistaken. Do not be hard on those who go astray; you yourself are just as liable to error. *Tom Jones* is, as has been shown, a book devised and shaped to drive this message home. But because this shape depends for its recognition on a reread-ing, in the strict etymological sense, a *re*-vision, St. Paul's image of heaven as the place where, for the first time, we truly see becomes strikingly pertinent: "For now we see through a glass darkly; but then face to face; now I know in part; but then shall I know even as also I am known" (1 Cor. 13:11–12). What could be more applicable to *Tom Jones*? St. Paul's words could be used to describe the difference between the first and second readings, between the dimly partial and the fully known.

6

Christening the Comedy

Has any writer of comparable stature ever suffered the same injustice as Fielding? He has been denounced for succeeding, found wanting for so brilliantly achieving what he set out to do, condemned, not because his performance is inept, but because it is superb. The form of his art is disparaged, not the failure of its execution; he does his splendid best, and fastidious critics sniff their disapproval.

Kermode dismisses this art, in the manner sanctioned by Dr. Johnson, by awarding the palm to the great rival, Richardson, whom he praises for drawing his breath in pain to tell the story (*Lit. Crit.*, 238). Fielding, of course, his style deliberately designed to frustrate too close an intimacy with his characters, their tribulations and inner turmoil, his narration aimed at keeping the reader coolly detached from the action, admittedly suffered no like anguish, no self-laceration, in telling *his* story. This is true; and if all storytelling is, as Kermode implies, a reenactment of Jacob's struggle with the dark angel, that long enervating wrestle through night until the self-discovery, the new naming of morning, then the dispute is over and Fielding's inferiority plain.

But Fielding neither tells nor wishes to tell that kind of story. His is a comic vision, stemming from the reiterated assurance of Genesis that God looked on his creation and found it good, as Tom's attack on the Man of the Hill's pessimism makes so admirably clear (431–32). Those who proclaim Fielding's inferiority to Richardson are often simply expressing a prejudice in favor of tragedy, a vote for pessimism, as the more mature, if harsher, interpretation of life, based on a brave confronting of experience rather than the fantasies of wish fulfillment. If only they said so instead of decrying Fielding's art for flouting their prejudice, no one could complain. As it is, objecting to Fielding because he is a comedian, with a style and narratology to match, is as foolish as it is futile: those who prefer the other kind of story should say so without turning it into a matter for self-congratulation.

Fielding criticism starts from the datum of his comic impulse, his euphoric conviction of an underlying rightness in things, his satisfaction with the material world, his sense of an ultimate harmony between man, nature, and society, akin to the final reconciliations of *The Winter's Tale*. We scour Fielding in vain for any radical disenchantment with things as they are, any revolutionary rage to raze the established order. Even in so basic a matter as the marriage of Tom and Sophia, this conserving, stabilizing temper is evident.

The early alleged affinities with the picaresque are mistaken and misleading. If, as is possible, the author of *Lazarillo* was a Jew, then the whole picaresque vision was first shaped by an outsider. Smollett, another outsider, a Scot in London, alien and disliked, could easily continue a fiction appropriate to someone living in uneasy toleration on the margins of established society. But Fielding was never an outsider, and Tom is a false picaro; he may occasionally talk the language of the castaway, the homeless, forsaken wanderer, but he is really the heir to Paradise Hall and the destined spouse of Sophia. Partridge, resolutely refusing to believe that Tom is in permanent exile, is foolishly right—what he wants to be true is finally true: Tom *shall* return home blessed and fortunate. (Don Quixote is not so happy in finding reality conform to his dreams.)

The contrast between Tom and Gatsby is instructive. Gatsby is Mr. Nobody from Nowhere and his disastrous end is the retaliation of established society on the upstart. Gatsby is doomed, tragic, whereas Tom is comic, fortune's child. If Tom *is* an adventurer, it is in the Pascalian sense of man as exiled king whose mission in life is to repossess his lost kingdom.[1] He may seem an outsider who can, at best, only dream of the golden girl on the golden mountain. He, the bastard, with no rightful position in the society that is opened to him only through Allworthy's grace—the foundling's fate would have been so different had Mrs. Wilkins's advice prevailed—has even less hope than Jimmy Gatz in his more mobile society of marrying a rich man's daughter. Sophia is wealthy enough in expectation to make her a match for Lord Fellamar; what hope has a penniless foundling of winning her? Only in fairy tales do such hypergamies occur; otherwise they are the brainstorms of vainglorious Malvolios. Western, we are told, would no more have considered marrying his daughter to a poor man than to an animal; for him the one mésalliance is as monstrous as the other (278).

The impossibility of the match is underscored by the fact that neither lover ever contemplates subverting the marriage norms of their society. Sophia's admirable rebellion against her father stops well short of an untrammeled insistence on the individual's right to choose a mate. She will defy him only to the point of refusing to be coerced into union with a man she abhors. She will not marry Blifil whatever her father says, but she will marry Tom only with her father's consent—indeed, in final, delightful affectation, only at his insistence.

Tom is no more antagonistic to society's norms than is Sophia. He sees her as impossibly beyond his reach; far from considering elopement, he shrinks from it in horror as an act that would distress Allworthy, betray Western, and ruin Sophia. Tom is far too principled to be an adventurer in the pejorative sense, is *ingénu* rather than manipulator. Not once does he express the revolutionary, antisocial view that love has rights superior to those of status or wealth. He despairingly accepts, without any reproach from the narrator, that Sophia cannot be his.

Yet the requirements of comedy insist that she must be his, and

Fielding's plot is designed to produce that happy consummation. Far from defying the marriage conventions of eighteenth-century England, Fielding reinforces them in the solution he contrives. The discovery of Tom's true identity raises him to the status of gentleman, wrong side of the blanket notwithstanding, and at the same time he decisively supplants Blifil as Allworthy's heir, making him for Western as desirable a son-in-law as he had previously been detestable. It is a conservative solution to the dilemma that leaves society as secure as ever. The nuptials of Tom and Sophia are as supportive of stability and tradition as those of Perdita and Florizel; in neither case, despite initial appearances, is the world turned upside down.

The matter is, of course, much more fundamental than a placid acceptance of marriage norms; Fielding's conservatism here betokens an underlying attitude to life in general. Lady Mary Wortley Montagu tells how she was especially saddened to hear of Fielding's death because she knew no man who enjoyed life so much (Rawson, 140). He is at home in the world, a defender of man, an advocate for existence, and his values are wholly, unashamedly secular. The little Anderson boy, in danger of dying, pronounces Fielding's credo: "I shan't die, God Almighty, I'm sure, won't take Tommy away; let heaven be ever so fine a place, I had rather stay here and starve with you and my papa, than go to it" (637). Out of the mouths of babes. Heaven is there, Fielding hopes, waiting for us when the time comes, and we do want to go there, but there is no rush: time enough when the journey can no longer be postponed. Meanwhile, there is a world to enjoy. At the close, Tom's homecoming complete, we are assured that he is "the happiest of all human kind: for what happiness this world affords equal to the possession of such a woman as Sophia, I sincerely own I have never yet discovered" (872). The personal note is unmistakable. Bunyan's road leads to the Celestial City; Fielding asks no higher felicity for Tom than the marriage bed with Sophia in it—that is *his* kind of consummation. Those who feel that such an aspiration is not exalted enough are profoundly out of sympathy with Fielding's conservative, unchiliastic temperament: his kingdom is of this world, here and now.

Dostoyevski called *Don Quixote* the saddest book of them all;[2]

Tom Jones must rank among the merriest, and the world, should it ever need defense counsel, could do no better than to retain Fielding. The reconciliation of the love affair with the marriage rules of his society signifies an ultimately joyful acceptance of the world, at least within his fiction, as a place where love and happiness, virtue and justice can all be simultaneously achieved. It is perhaps the last time that a major novelist will make such a breathtaking claim. *Tom Jones* has been seen as the last joyous product of a conviction that all the essential impulses of a good man can be happily harmonized with one another, none of his innate tendencies necessarily clashing with the rest; love and honor, faith and reason, Providence and fortune, are, for the final time, made to appear complementary.[3] The work shines with the brilliance of a star just before implosion. Harmony will soon be shattered in the emergence of a series of necessary oppositions: individual versus society, religion versus science, thought versus feeling, impulse versus principle. In Fielding all dichotomies are reconciled; from our own ruptured, splintered age we survey *Tom Jones* with nostalgic envy.

Even in his own time, of course, Fielding's blithe evangel was severely challenged, notably by his great competitor, Richardson, in his opposing masterpiece, *Clarissa*. *Clarissa* contradicts *Tom Jones* by depicting the world as a fallen place from which the virtuous soul, raped and crucified, can escape only through death. These two masterworks of eighteenth-century fiction exhibit not the difference in talent that Dr. Johnson claimed to detect but radically opposed conceptions of art and life.[4] Both are fictional representations of the Christian epic, following the soul's journey through tribulation and testing to final reward, but the tragic mode of the one is in sharp contrast to the comic mode of the other. Clarissa, like Bunyan's hero, must repudiate family and society before being united with her heavenly Father in death. Her temporal world is a snare, vicious and unredeemed, no fit habitation for the Christian soul. The pattern of her life—mortification, atonement, redemption—is an imitation of Christ, a *via dolorosa;* her quest is ultimately transcendental, and, as the bride of Christ, she belongs to hagiography at least as much as to social history.

Tom Jones, by contrast, finds *his* salvation in and through the things of this world, its social habits and institutions; there is no irreconcilable division between soul and body, spirit and world, as there so remorselessly is in *Clarissa*. Like Christ before her, Clarissa is a worldly failure so that she may be a spiritual success; Fielding, eluding that dichotomy too, has Tom find redemption here and now, as he acquires wisdom, virtue, and happiness in this world through the discovery of his true social self as Allworthy's heir and Sophia's husband. Richardson's is a transcendental, Fielding's an immanent, solution; in the one, world and spirit, society and virtue, are incompatible; in the other, the triumph of goodness is certified through earthly forms and social institutions. Death is Clarissa's goal, marriage, Tom's.

The unspoken but unmistakable comic contract between narrator and reader in *Tom Jones* should prevent the latter from going astray during the incest episode. Even when Tom takes himself so seriously as to don the mantle of Oedipus, the reader knows better. The controlling comic context forbids us to invest the hero in tragic robes, with his very name serving as a reassurance: how could a man called Tom Jones be the peer of Oedipus or Agamemnon? Arthur Miller, challenging Aristotelian norms, proposes a Willy Loman as his tragic hero, but Fielding throws down no gauntlet to hierarchical decorum: the Joneses do not belong to the same tragic stock as the house of Atreus.

We are encouraged to go further: surely a man so named must end up happy? We would feel cheated if he really did turn out to be an Augustan Oedipus or a candidate for Tyburn, could with every reason reproach the narrator for so brutally betraying our comic contract. Tom Jones is the comic hero who finally comes home, happy and prosperous, to his father's house, Clarissa the tragic heroine who escapes the prison of this world to receive her eternal reward in paradise. For Richardson facts are symbols and the material world is subjected to a spiritual interpretation. Clarissa in her barred bedroom is an image of the soul immured in the body—"this suffering angel" in "so damned a nook."[5] Tom in prison, by contrast, is just a miserable man, admittedly so woebegone that even Thwackum might have pitied him, but there is no hint of a war between God and Satan—Thwackum is no demon, just a nasty man (776). With Fielding we are securely in the empirical world. No doubt Sophia is, as her name attests, wisdom, and the marriage with Tom may well suggest the metaphorical union of wisdom and energy, with all the wholesome consequences that flow from it; but, primarily, the marriage is between an exuberant young man and a beautiful, spirited girl, and its chief products will be two children. Allegory takes a back seat to the primary facts of human existence and, for Fielding, these facts are essentially comic.

It is, moreover, the comedy of certainty, thereby affronting our modern pieties, our conventional wisdom, about the nature of the novel. The novel, in Kundera's skeptical formulation, is the territory where no one, neither Anna nor Karenin, possesses the truth.[6] Its wisdom is the wisdom of uncertainty. It seeks above all (and this is its chief value) to reject the craving of fanatics and ideologues for certitude, for the one, clear, unmistakable, unchallengeable truth. Hence its preference for ambiguity, relativity, the either-or attitude that is the foe of apodictic, dogmatic discourse. Reality is unknowable, the world a mystery, the novel the affirmation of that inexplicability. Its great hero is Cervantes, who, following God's farewell to the world as its supreme director, first exposed its resultant fearsome ambiguity. Cervantes saw that God's removal meant that there was no longer a single divine truth, but instead myriad, relative truths to match the number of participants and observers. The world becomes a vast ambiguity, a welter of contradictory and incompatible truths—windmills and giants, sheep and armies, basins and helmets; the novel becomes what Georg Lukács calls it, the epic of a world abandoned by God.[7] Hence the pointlessness of seeking in *Don Quixote* a moral position when it only offers a metaphysical impasse; *Don Quixote* asks but does not answer questions. This is the legacy of Cervantes: the impossibility of knowing, the elusiveness of truth.[8]

It will be at once apparent how totally inapplicable all this is to *Tom Jones*. If Kundera is right, either *Tom Jones* is not a novel or it is a novel that eludes his formula of skepticism. Tom as Blifil's adversary does possess the truth. More important, behind Tom stands a narrator in even more abundant possession of the truth. Most important of all, behind the knowing narrator is the God of creation, the supreme novelist, omniscient and infallible, whose work is the world and whose characters we all are, guaranteeing both the structures of certainty and the final, felicitous outcome of history. If behind Cervantes is the shock of abandonment, the sense of instability and disorientation, behind Fielding is an assurance of presence and the promise of an intelligible, moral universe where, temporary mishaps notwithstanding, all shall be well.

Far from a sense of abandonment, some readers resent in Fielding the continual authorial intrusions with their reassuring tone; they object to being too stiflingly, too fussily, cared for—if only this too providential author would leave us to our own resources. Nor is there in Fielding any metaphysical anguish, any identity crisis such as afflicts Cervantes' tragic protagonist, but rather the confidence of the Gospel assurance that all shall be revealed and made intelligible in time—and in time to save us. "I make not the least doubt, but time will shew all matters in their true and natural colours" (799). Mrs. Miller expresses the epistemological optimism that she shares with her creator. *Tom Jones* deals in certainties: the reader knows exactly who the characters are and what they stand for. Don Quixote is the mock hero, knight of the sorrowful countenance whose generous attempts to redeem the world end repeatedly in wasteful absurdity. Tom Jones is the comic hero, a true knight-errant who preserves Mrs. Waters from murder, the Anderson family from starvation, and Nancy from ruin. Mrs. Miller, an Augustan lady, calls him an angel of mercy; in medieval times she might as easily have called him her own true knight (689).

Tom Jones, moreover, does answer questions, the moral ones triumphantly, while the metaphysical ones are not even considered because the answers are taken for granted: the world makes sense because it is God's handiwork. Fielding as author speaks, in turn, with the author-ity of the creator, the God of his work, and, as such, its infallible expositor. He knows the truth, and if we read on trustingly, we, too, shall know it. His novel replicates God's providential plan and predicts our eventual destiny: all shall be well. As Fielding, in his creation, disposes the fates of Tom and Blifil, so God, in his supreme fiction, will decide the destinies of elect and reprobate. Fielding, in his art, reprieves us from that state of unknowing that is, for Kundera, the inescapable human condition. "You shall be like gods": Fielding's fiction, though not in any impious or blasphemous way, repeats the serpent's promise; transiently, within his pages, we shall know as God knows.

Herein lies Fielding's unique contribution to the novel, his unrepeatable legacy. He restores what Cervantes calls into question, employing the new, ambiguous genre—the work of man in which, unlike the epic, God may not appear—to propose an old-fashioned, conservative view of the world as stable, secure, protected. The contrast between the respective puppet shows in both novels makes this clear. In *Don Quixote* the show exposes the metaphysical bewilderment, the existential anguish, of the hero who assaults the Moorish puppetry because representation starts to resemble imagination too closely: the racial enemies, the foes inside the skull, the wooden figures, all are bafflingly confounded; fantasy and truth are indistinguishable for Quixote, and the metaphysical deeps gape for us, too.[9] In *Tom Jones* there is no hint of the abyss; the puppet show is used simply to ridicule a pompously mistaken attempt to turn an innocent entertainment into a didactic art, and the whole episode is aimed at helping us to recognize a social truth, not to instill in us an unsettling metaphysical doubt (567–68).

Cervantes no longer knows what nature is—there may simply be a succession of masks with no true face behind them; hence the greatness of the novel in giving expression to this sense of profound insecurity. For Fielding, by contrast, the ubiquitous role-playing is simply part of a repertoire of human chicanery; less our contemporary than Cervantes in this respect, Fielding is cheerfully confident of nature—there is always a face behind the mask, waiting to be revealed. Nature will out, however many and devious the deceivers. Fielding knows no metaphysical uncertainty about identity; despite his ignorance of his birth, Tom suffers no crisis comparable to that of Cervantes' hero, and far from agonizing over the mystery of his parentage, Tom simply gets on with enjoying his life, a far cry from Oedipus. Cervantes is our brother, promoter and partner of our anxieties, but Fielding, so old-fashioned by comparison, may be a better friend and a surer guide.

This archaism is reflected in his reunification of the two elements sundered in Cervantes: adventure and assurance. Although Fielding's world is as hazardous and unpredictable as the Spaniard's, it is one that we know his hero will master. This very form of *Tom Jones* conveys this sense of security. In art, form is always more than a form. Every significant novel offers some solution to the problem of the meaning of life, and it does so as much through its form as its content; both together constitute an inviolable, meaningful whole. Fielding's answer (for us it is almost an oxymoron) is that life is an adventure that ends happily. He clearly savored the extraordinary charms of action; one need only contrast the pent-up, claustrophobic, voyeuristic art of Richardson. All is activity in Fielding, not simply in the middle section of *Tom Jones,* where the horses race from one inn, one contretemps, to another, but throughout the novel. Coexisting with this, surprisingly for us for whom adventure has come to mean what happens to Pip or Emma Bovary or Anna Karenina or Kafka's land surveyor—something that ends in frustration or death—is the blithe assurance, implicit in the form of Fielding's tale, that this adventure must end in happiness.

For Fielding tragedy is simply uncompleted comedy, a story halted too soon. It is true, but it is partial, incomplete. Alyosha in *The Brothers Karamazov* does not deny what Ivan says; he simply objects that Ivan has not told the whole truth.[10] Aldous Huxley praises Fielding for telling the whole truth, though he means it in a different sense from the argument of this chapter. He is referring to the incident in which Sophia has the embarrassing fall that results in the exposure of her charming posterior, the implication being that this, however lifelike, could never happen to Phaedra or Cordelia or to any other member of the tragic sisterhood.[11] True, Sophia horrifies Honour with her assertion that she will stab herself to the heart rather than become Blifil's wife, but this simply reveals, apart from a brave spirit, a complete misunderstanding of her assigned role, on a par with Tom's misappraisal of himself as Oedipus (320). She may possess the resolve to execute her dreadful threat, but there is no need for such drastic measures in a work by Fielding. It is in this radical Christian sense, not just in the revealing of the heroine's backside, that Fielding tells the whole truth, the complete story. And this story is, of course, a gospel, a good story, a comedy—a fact equally perceptible in what he says and how he says it. The assurance is that of the great, magisterial comedians, of Dame Julian, of Prospero: all shall be well; tell your piteous heart there's no harm done.[12] Narrator and narrative, style and meaning, form and content reinforce each other; Fielding's dramatic projection of himself in his novel provides a kind of comic analogue of the true believer's reliance on a benign providence in real life. The narrator watches lovingly over his fiction as God over his world, and all fears of Tyburn, incest, suicide are void and vain. It is required you do awake your faith:[13] Paulina's exhortation is propaedeutic to a right reading of Fielding's masterpiece.

To appreciate Fielding we must have faith, must believe in the goodness of this world. Tom has the author fully behind him in his dispute with the Old Man of the Hill. Fielding is the great comedian, the last complete comedian in European literature; after him, there occurs a desecration, an undermining of comedy, at the very least a radical revision. Tragedy, says Kundera, brings us consolation by providing us with the lovely illusion of human greatness: "The comic is crueler; it brutally reveals the meaninglessness of everything." Clearly, this refers to Kafka, Ionesco, Beckett; it could not be more misleading when applied to Chaucer, Rabelais, or Fielding. The world of the complete, of the "pure" comedians is replete with meaning, charged with joy and vitality. Kundera acknowledges this in his description of the decline of European laughter:

> For Rabelais, the merry and the comic were still one and the same. In the eighteenth century, the humour of Sterne and Diderot is an affectionate, nostalgic recollection of Rabelaisian merriment. In the nineteenth century, Gogol is a melancholy humorist: "The longer

and more carefully we look at a funny story, the sadder it becomes,"
said he. Europe has looked for such a long time at the funny side
of its own existence that in the twentieth century, Rabelais' merry
epic has turned into the despairing comedy of Ionesco, who says,
"There's only a thin line between the horrible and the comic." The
European history of laughter comes to an end.[14]

If this is as true as it depressingly seems, it becomes all the more important to ponder the work of our last true comedian, the heir of
Chaucer and Rabelais, and to ask ourselves how in him the feat was
accomplished. The remaining pages address this question.

What must be summarily dismissed is the foolish notion that
Fielding is a comedian because he is a Polyanna-type optimist. Behind
the myth of the carefree roisterer is the clear-eyed observer of human
folly and malice; one glance at the opening page of *A Voyage to Lisbon* should suffice to dispel the canard of the fatuously cheerful optimist. In life Fielding knew only too well that the Blifils win and the
Toms go under. The question remains: Why is he so cheerful? Any
sensible answer will be that it was despite what he knew of men and
life. His comedy is an act of faith, a decision of the will. He is a comedian not because he is complacent but because he is Christian. The
paradox is inescapable. This comedy, created by the most worldly of
men, the most secular of writers, is inconceivable without its religious
infrastructure, its spiritual guarantees: "no God, no comedy" is the
slogan at the entrance to this fiction. Heaven can wait, but, far more
important, heaven does wait, does much more than just wait. The
undeniable secular values are just as undeniably, on inspection, deri-
vations from Christianity, sustained and, in the end, sustainable only
by a religious assurance. Underwriting the idea of a comic world is the
Judeo-Christian interpretation of life from Genesis to Incarnation, and
Fielding is its last, complete exponent.

Consider some of the ostensibly damaging allegations leveled at
Fielding: that he is too dismissive of the worth of suspicion as an element in the moral life; that he underrates the value of prudence; that
he is deplorably lax toward sin and sinners; that he indulges in Tom

the same moral failings that he shared with his wastrel hero. A glance at the pages of his detractors from Richardson and Dr. Johnson onward reveals that all of this has been adduced as evidence of a careless, irresponsible man with a frivolously flawed outlook on life. In fact, tracked to their source, these attitudes are seen to be the proofs of a fundamentally Christian temperament, finding its natural, orthodox expression in an equally fundamental comic vision of life. For Fielding, as for Chaucer, comedy and Christianity are natural allies, each telling a happy tale of deliverance—Fielding's is a christened comedy. We may, if we insist, go on faulting his beliefs and attitudes provided we recognize their provenance; if Fielding is careless and culpable, it is because the Christian legacy as inherited and interpreted by him entails a similar heedlessness, a blessed self-forgetting. He dislikes suspicion because he suspects it as the sign of a bad mind, of a complicity with evil; he is uneasy about prudence because it is the trade name of a shrewd selfishness; he does not rage against sinners, even those as wicked as Blifil, because he regards them as dolts, however devious—the more calculating, the more foolish; he approves Tom's reckless self-disregard because it seems to him a secularized equivalent of certain key Christian insights—of taking no heed for the morrow, of losing one's life in order to save it.

It is a fallacy, more reprehensible in us than in Richardson, to regard Richardson as a Christian, Fielding as an anti-Christian, writer. They are both Christian writers. Confusion arises from a failure to distinguish the double inheritance of Christian teaching, the two divergent moral traditions discernible even in the Gospels, fortified by two opposing sets of parables and exempla. There are the parables of prudence—the talents, the unjust steward, the wise and foolish virgins—parables of management and mismanagement, exhorting us to be vigilant, to take care, to make provision, to exercise forethought, to be, above all, each one of us, individually responsible for his or her own salvation, to be laudably selfish. These are at the root of Richardson's concept of the good life: a cautious and watchful discipline.

Fielding, by contrast, finds his inspiration in the opposing parables of self-forgetting: the lilies of the field and their exemplary improvidence, the reiterated injunction not to be forever fretting over the doubtful future but to trust in God, the insistence that only those who lose life will find it, the promise that if we seek righteousness alone, then all the other good things will follow. These parables recommend not a becoming but a being, not a striving but a repose, not a vigilant egoism but a holy heedlessness: stop worrying, all is well. If, as Georges Bernanos says, grace is to forget oneself, then Tom, with all his shortcomings, may sooner enter the kingdom than those watchful egotists Pamela and Clarissa.[15]

The triumph of the prudential virtues, which harmonized well with the eighteenth-century view of Christianity as rational self-interest, meant that the virtues espoused by Fielding's fiction were bound to be misconstrued or overlooked. Consequently, the attack on him transcends his alleged laxity toward individual sinners to become a denunciation of his attitude to life and of the artistic form he devised to dramatize this. Cobbett's remarks about the moral subversiveness of *Tom Jones* had already been anticipated by Lady Mary Wortley Montagu, who rebuked Fielding for encouraging an optimistic abandon in young people, a criminal assurance that they could launch into love without thought of the consequences or prudent provision for the future, a charge repeated in our own times by Ford Madox Ford (Rawson, 132, 348). Dr. Johnson similarly complained that Fielding's rogue hero was a bad model for the young (Rawson, 115–16), much as people today deplore the behavior of pop stars as likely to lead their idolatrously imitative followers astray. What most angers Lady Mary is that Fielding fosters improvidence among the young, inciting them to marry for love with no heed to the hazardous future and the indispensable income; as a wealthy woman she doubtless resented the fact that people like herself so often had to pick up the tab for the irresponsibilities of younger relatives. Fielding was, for her, a false teacher, a seducer of the young. Despite his protest that he did not slight prudence, despite his insistence that his work champions nature against romance, Lady Mary attacks him for subordinating nature to fairy tale and its happy-ever-after mentality.

The truth is that Fielding's work exhibits a secularized Christian hope, a trust in Providence rather than a predilection for fairy tale—the lilies of the field neither strive nor fret, and yet are more splendid than Solomon. Worry is a kind of atheism, a disbelief in God's promise, for, if even the sparrows are sheltered, it is a sin to fear calamity. It is required you do awake your faith. Fielding's work domesticates the Providence of God within Augustan England. Tom Jones, despite his thoughtlessness, will not be lost, because he is in Fielding's keeping. And so, when the narrator speculates that Tom may end on the gallows, that particular fate is at once foreclosed; whatever else happens, Tom will not be hanged. The reader trusts the narrator as the believer trusts God, and confidently remits the comic resolution to him: all shall be well.

Moreover, Fielding loves Tom for the very qualities that Lady Mary condemns. Tom is another lily of the field, thoughtless and improvident, the complete opposite of the precise, calculating Blifil, forever craftily taking thought of the morrow and of the day after it. It is because Tom does not seek a reward that Fielding makes sure he gets one: those who do not care will be cared for, those who care overmuch will lose both the prize and themselves. Again, the secret is related to the secularization of a religious idea: first seek the kingdom and all things shall be added unto you. The good will be happy because they put goodness before happiness, the hedonists will miss happiness and everything else. This is the central Christian paradox. Certainly, Fielding's kingdom is of this world and his values are, at bottom, thoroughly humanist and social: friendship, good nature, generosity, love and the rest. Tom in his marriage bed is in heaven, not preparing for it, and he is there because he has not plotted to obtain it, has, if anything, come recklessly close to throwing it away. But only he who loses his life will save it. Improbable though it seems at first glance, the drunken womanizer who outraged Dr. Johnson, "the fellow that sells himself," in Thackeray's scornful dismissal, Lady Bellaston's gigolo, the Augustan Midnight Cowboy, is the secularized embodiment of this key Christian belief.[16] Blifil, by contrast, is a loser at last *because* he is obsessed with winning. Fielding's humanism will not properly be appreciated by those who miss how rooted it is in Christianity.

Fielding's humanist paradox makes sense only in the context of its Christian derivation, for otherwise there would be in him an irreconcilable conflict between the impulse to show goodness as its own reward—hence to condemn any form of egotistic calculation—and the even stronger compulsion to create comic masterpieces. Tragedy suggests itself as the more appropriate medium for the first impulse; clearly, the goodness of Cordelia is its own reward, because it is so bleakly her only one. But, for the Christian, *King Lear* is an unfinished story, an incomplete comedy because it fails to show the resurrected Cordelia translated to beatitude. Fielding is a comedian; all his heroes end up united or reunited in marital bliss with the women they love; nothing is here for tears. The calculators will fail while the spontaneously openhanded will be rewarded; generosity is the best policy provided it is not a policy—this is Fielding's paradox. The young hero in the fairy tale wins golden girl and golden mountain because he treats the old crone, in reality the queen of the fairies, with respect and kindness; his competitors are discomfited because they are rude and selfish to an apparently insignificant old woman. Nobody, of course, knows at the time her true identity; it is just that the good man is instinctively, naturally good, while the bad man has to be bribed to act decently: no bribe, no decency.

But it would be perverse to say that the moral is that we should treat kindly the next old crone we meet on the long shot that she might be the queen of the fairies—that would be to degrade a gratuitous, altruistic act into a piece of strategic calculation. Every old woman should be treated as if she were the queen of the fairies, because, in the root Christian sense, every old woman is. Jesus makes this clear when he answers his puzzled interlocutors, mystified at being praised for having helped him: "When you did this unto the least of these my brethren, you did it unto me." The converse is just as fearfully true: to turn away in contempt from the wretched of the earth is to reject Christ. Those who go about sharp-eyed to help the important and influential, while leaving the helpless to rot, are not good men but good strategists. Tom Jones is, to his credit, no strategist at all; that is why he is a winner.

Blessings come to him as a consequence of his impulsive,

sometimes reckless, even (for a certain kind of moralist) culpable generosity. His urge to make amends to Molly for, as he mistakenly thinks, letting her down sends him to her room, where he catches her with Square and then learns about Will Barnes as her original seducer (213). Doing the generous thing gets him off the hook, but his release is the felicitious by-product of his magnanimity, not its willed intention. He owes his ultimate success to two factors: his own natural goodness and his role within a Fielding comedy. The Lord was with Joseph and he was a lucky fellow; Fielding is with Tom Jones and he is equally lucky, but the paradox is that he deserves his good fortune.

"To be sure it is never good to pass by an old woman without giving her something, especially if she looks at you" (666, also 561, 589). Partridge supplies his own superstitiously craven rationale for charity. The giveaway is in the final clause; Partridge gives out of fear, as a placatory, propitiatory gesture. The old woman may be a witch who will curse you for your neglect; if Partridge could be sure she were harmless, he would spurn her. It is the selfishness of fear—the selfishness of hope advises charity because she may be the queen of the fairies—but hope or fear, queen or witch, reward or curse, it is the same selfishness whether it take the form of an insurance against disaster or an investment for future prosperity. Tom's giving has nothing to do with personal hopes or fears; it is an instinctive, uncalculating reaction to another's distress. "Happy is he whom the dangers of others makes cautious" (574). Again, Partridge is the oracle, and some critics, admittedly with the apparent support of the narrator himself (579), find here the clue to the book's meaning. *Tom Jones* is proposed as a cautionary tale in which the hero blessedly and at last learns the prudence whose lack is so hurtful throughout his career. Other readers will find it hard to accept that the aim of *Tom Jones* is to teach the hero to imitate the villain. The ordinary reader surely leaves the book less imbued with the desirability of prudence than uplifted by the splendor of generosity.

If you give you will be rewarded, so long as the giving is not for the sake of the reward. The pattern is too consistent throughout *Tom Jones* to be random, mere coincidence; we are clearly in the realm of

Christian Providence, not of pagan *fortuna*. Driven by generous guilt, Tom goes to Molly's house and is released from his moral dilemma. Against Partridge's remonstrances, he gives a shilling to the beggar and is immediately rewarded with the presentation of Sophia's lost pocketbook (561). He overpowers the assailant of the Merry-Andrew—he always instinctively sides with the underdog—and the rescuee at once blurts out the vital information about Sophia's movements and whereabouts (576–77). With Partridge screaming in his ear to kill the foiled highwayman, Tom not only spares but succors him (604–605). The man turns out to be the relative of Mrs. Miller, and she will become one of Tom's most strenuous partisans and powerful character witnesses with Allworthy at the book's climax. Tom saves Nightingale from a beating, and Nightingale becomes the friend who devises the plan—for a time it seems a blunder, but in the end it works—for detaching Tom from Lady Bellaston (621–22). Amid the troubles of his own chaotic life, Tom intervenes to save Nancy from ruin and her family from disgrace, and, once again, Mrs. Miller argues fervently for the preserver of her family against the calumnies of Blifil.

Most crucial of all for its influence upon the final *peripeteia*, Tom, at great risk to himself, "without the least apprehension or concern for his own safety," rushes to the assistance of Mrs. Waters and prevents her murder (440). His reckless courage is highlighted the more by the contrasting conduct of the Man of the Hill, who sits, a misanthropic dropout, with a gun in his hand throughout the struggle. In the conventional idiom of the Augustan gallant, Tom deprecates the lady's expressions of gratitude by telling her that "Heaven seemed to have designed him as the happy instrument of her protection" (441). In this Christian comedy the cliché is gospel truth. The interval between act and reward is greater than in the incidents with the beggar and the Merry-Andrew, but the same pattern is even more dramatically demonstrated, though the correlation must await the book's climax. Heaven *has* sent Tom to save Mrs. Waters, regardless of what happens later in the bedroom at Upton. In all England there are only three living people who know the secret of Tom's birth, and two of these, Blifil and Dowling, are in league to keep it hidden; only Mrs.

Waters can reveal the truth, and that only because Tom has earlier saved her life. Had he selfishly left her to die, it would have been to his own eventual destruction. Tom's folly in exposing himself to danger is another confirmation of the Christian paradox that only he who loses his life will save it. Truly, the bread cast by Tom on the waters comes back a hundredfold, but the thrower must throw without wanting or even thinking of a return.

The book celebrates imprudence, extols a splendid recklessness, not a careful calculation. You are not to sit by the tide in eager expectation of the massive dividends floating toward you from your earlier investments. Blifil is the shrewd exponent of the capitalist virtues who schemes, plans, anticipates—and fails. He is the book's Narcissus, salient example of hermetic self-love in its pages, with all the shortcomings that Fielding, anticipating Freud, finds within that temperament. There is a nice irony in the fact that Aldous Huxley, in his utopian novel *Island,* should have his hero light on *Tom Jones* as manifesto of sexual liberation in his struggle against hellfire, Calvinist repression, particularly in that the form his emancipation takes is that of masturbation; ironic, because there are grounds for believing that Blifil, the book's villain, is himself a masturbator, and that the two roles are intimately linked in Fielding's mind.[17] Explaining Blifil's apparent insensitivity to Sophia's charms, Fielding tells us that it is not because of any aversion to women, "but his appetites were, by nature, so moderate that he was easily able, by philosophy or by study, or by some other method, to subdue them" (263). The reader is left to speculate as to what this "other method" might be. Masturbation would fit in neatly with Blifil's personality, especially if we remember Woody Allen's definition: sex with someone I love. If true, it provides yet another contrast between hero and villain, between the reckless spender of himself, lover of others, and the cautious hoarder, keeping things to himself, cherishing only himself. Self-love, for Fielding, is a weakness, a sign of disease, not of health. Tom, immersed in personal problems, can forget himself in order to help others—the Andersons, the Millers, Nightingale, Mrs. Waters, beggars, Merry-Andrews. It seems strange of Thackeray to blame Fielding for treating Tom too leniently.

Is there a better Christian in the book, Allworthy included? Allworthy rebukes Tom at the end for being too forgiving, but any such indictment will have to include Christ too, for where in the Gospels does he adopt the Allworthy line that we can have too much of a good thing? Fielding ironically contrasts the weakness of compassion with the nobility of egoism, that exemplary firmness of mind which enables a man to roll through the world like a polished bowl, "without being once stopped by the calamities which happen to others" (673). The weakling cares for others, the strong man for himself. But by their fruits you shall know them—it is the supreme comic promise. At the end the compassionate man has triumphed, the egotist is ruined: what seemed weakness is strength, what seemed power is impotence.

Compassion should, ideally, be unconscious. One should do good like a burglar, or, better still, like a sleepwalker. The self-forgetful Allworthy, standing in his shirt, is an image of salvation. In the preface Lyttleton is rebuked in what is really the supreme Fielding compliment: "there are certain actions of which you are apt to be extremely forgetful"—namely, his acts of benevolence (35). The Gospel injunction to do good stealthily is extended to forgetfully; we are to hoodwink not only onlookers but also ourselves by not allowing the left hand to know what the right hand is up to. The good man conceals his benefactions as the rascal does his depredations, shunning applause as the latter shuns censure. The best man has reached the highest stage of all, doing good without knowing it, instinctively, by reflex. It is not just a matter of keeping the other hand in the dark; the cerebral cortex itself is to be kept incommunicado. At the other extreme stand the Pharisees, the showmen of virtue, the thespians of goodness, performers randy for applause. Because it is applause they love, they get it, at least for a time: "I tell you, they have had their reward." But the solid, eternal satisfactions of heaven are reserved for the shy do-gooders. *Tom Jones* replicates, in its worldly way, the eschatological promise. That outstanding young man, Blifil, ostensibly so respectable, wins his temporary plaudits, but it is the truly good man, Tom, who at last inherits the kingdom.

This also explains what might otherwise be criticized as an

irresponsibly frivolous attitude to wrongdoers like Blifil. Some readers feel that Blifil gets off too easily at the end, though others might reply that to be left irredeemably Blifil, forever fated to scheme and fail, is surely punishment enough. Let Gryll be Gryll. If Fielding is soft on sinners, it is because they are hard on themselves. The old Jewish proverb says, when man thinks, God laughs. Fielding knew, if not the proverb, certainly the sentiment behind it. There is a long tradition in Judeo-Christian thought from the Psalms onward of the wise being fools in the eyes of God: *perdam sapientiam sapientiae;* unless you become as little children you cannot enter the kingdom. But if God laughs at the wise, what must be the divine convulsions when he contemplates the crafty? The devil is an ass. In *Paradise Lost,* Father and Son look down from heaven in amusement at the foolish antics of the self-important Satan, deluding himself that he is the feared foe of omnipotence.[18] The idea of the crafty cretin is equally fundamental in Fielding.

To critics who complain of his nonchalance toward sin, Fielding might have answered, Why fret over the misdeeds of the ungodly when the poor fools are finally their own worst enemies, no better than blunderers and buffoons? The rascally Blifils are, *because* of their devious machinations, a family of dolts, losers to a man. The Doctor, conspiring his brother's infiltration into Paradise Hall, inadvertently contrives his own expulsion. The Captain, plotting marriage to Allworthy's sister for the love of Allworthy's fortune, ironically provides the most stunningly dramatic instance of the imbecility of evil in this or any other book. Why does God laugh when man thinks? Because man thinks he is irrefutably right when he is hopelessly wrong; because man, living an adventure, would make it a blueprint; because a creature at the hazard of the present moment absurdly plans a future that will never be; in a word, because man dreams of the future but dies in the present. Thou fool, this night I require thy soul of thee. If God laughs, man trembles: such comedy is, for him, no laughing matter.

The two chapters dealing with the Captain's sudden death are a tour de force of black comedy, from the opening title—"A Receipt to regain the lost Affections of a Wife, which hath never been known to fail in the most desperate Cases"—to the final, mendacious epitaph (113–19). Fielding's predilection for parable is again evident—behind the Captain stands the figure of Christ's fool—and there is an almost cruel relish discernible beneath the bogus lamentations of the tongue-in-cheek narrator. What a pity that the Captain's most excellent plan for the long and costly renovation of Allworthy's estate cannot be presented—so keens the narrator; yet, far from being grief-stricken, he seems to be enjoying himself (113–14). Had we but world enough and time: the Captain is sure of both commodities. He knows that his own health is excellent and that Allworthy is an older man; it follows that he must one day inherit Allworthy's fortune. The great plan stands poised for Allworthy's death, and the actuarial Captain, satisfied of that imminent probability, pants to begin the work, when "he himself—died of an apoplexy" (114). The delight concentrated in that sudden punctuation mark almost leaps from the page. Impudent, idiot man, calculating the death of others, dies himself. Fielding ironically recites the litany of the Captain's calamity—"unlucky . . . unseasonable . . . malice of Fortune"—but fortune has nothing to do with God's decree. Life is unpredictable; woe, deserved woe, to the fool who thinks that it can be fixed within his Filofax. We end with a grim joke: the clown who dreamed of a great estate dies and receives the allotted six feet of earth that is every man's ultimate destiny, "adequate to all his future purposes" (114). *How Much Land Does a Man Need?* So asked Tolstoy in what Joyce called the greatest short story ever written. To this essentially religious question, the allegedly worldly Fielding—so coarse, so vulgarly hedonist, if we are to believe his detractors—supplies an answer as morally stringent, as tensely dramatic, as anything we shall find in the Gospels, in Pascal or Tolstoy. The accompanying levity intensifies rather than dilutes the seriousness of the whole episode.

Nor is this simply the sudden death that may overtake anyone of us, saint or sinner, sage or dunce; this is the fitting end to the sinful arrogance of the imbecile schemer. Bad enough to be a sinner of the flesh, foolishly licensing the undisciplined body to have its way at the expense of the endangered soul; how much more insensate to be a sinner of the mind, bartering one's salvation for a mirage, a non-existent future. In Tolstoy's story men die because they are too greedy; they kill themselves through their own exorbitant exertions, would live otherwise. But Fielding's fool dies taking a stroll in a garden, his only exertion a dream of the future, killed by God: this night I require thy soul of thee. It is more terrifying than Tolstoy, because it is only the dream, not the death, that is avoidable. And so comedy cedes to gravity, since every death, even the fool's, is finally a serious business; there is no levity when we at last contemplate the corpse of the calculator: "Death, that inexorable judge, had passed sentence on him, and refused to grant him a reprieve" (116–17).

The thematic importance of the episode is manifest as a rehearsal for the novel's major action. Like father, like son; why should the son succeed where the father so spectacularly fails? Fortune may be "a tender parent" (80), but in the end she is fickle and unreliable; Providence is the safer guardian. The Captain's plans flourish for a time, but are sure to founder at last. The Christian paradox is confirmed: the devil is cunning and powerful, yet is also feeble and foolish. And so the narrator prays for a right response to the tricks of the wicked: "Remove that mist which dims the intellects of mortals, and causes them to adore men for their art, or to detest them for their cunning in deceiving others, when they are, in reality, the objects only of ridicule, for deceiving themselves" (608). We must not admire rogues, but, just as surely, we are not to fear them, for they are simply fools. Here is the secret of Fielding's good humor in the face of wickedness: not an irresponsible levity, much less, as his detractors allege, a prejudice against virtue, a complicity with immorality, but a remarkable faith, unequaled in most of the Christians who condemn him, in the ultimate goodness of creation. The good win, the wicked fail: the ages of faith will be hard pressed to muster so confident a believer.

Good people, says Fielding, are too sensible to be wicked; far from addition or advantage, it is a diminution, a self-mutilation (328). All the prudence in the world will not save the bad man—a rug falls and a strategic seducer is exposed. Nor will imprudence destroy the good man—it may make his road more difficult, but it will not alter his destination. Evil, however guarded, is finally self-destructive. The wicked do their worst and in the end blessings flow from it. Tom incautiously tells Blifil about Black George's part in the poaching, and Blifil maliciously betrays him to the tutors, who, in turn, rush to tell Allworthy. The irony is that Tom would have been thrashed but for Blifil's treachery, because Allworthy now issues fresh orders that Tom is not to be beaten: to have suffered so nobly in order to protect a friend deserves praise rather than punishment, declares Allworthy, to the chagrin of the thwarted, scandalized tutors (133). Blifil tries to hurt Tom and, in fact, saves him, in what is Fielding's domestic rendition of the *felix culpa*. The devil, bent on ruining mankind in Eden, merely ensures the Redeemer's arrival. Evil lacks imagination, is unable to see beyond its own corrupt nose. Allworthy's illness provides yet another instance of the *felix culpa;* at the time apparently so unfortunate, it really gives Blifil the opportunity to be wicked, supplying him with the rope to hang himself. As a result, he is finally exposed as a rogue and Tom left the single, unchallenged heir. Things could not have worked out better and the villain has contributed to the happy consummation.

His conviction of the stupidity of evil is what so sharply differentiates Fielding from the Orwell of *Nineteen Eighty-four*. For Orwell, good is a fragile thing, perilously existing within a matrix of omnipotent evil, just as the lovers' refuge is a room within Oceania. Winston admires the torturer O'Brien as a superman, as the possessor of a mind that includes and is greater than Winston's own: evil is intelligent. In Fielding the situation is reversed: evil is smaller than good, can, at most, hope to live concealed within it, just as Winston vainly hopes to live undetected within Oceania. Blifil stupidly "fancied he knew Jones to the bottom," but knows only himself: how can evil comprehend good? That Blifil should despise Tom for not being more attached to his own interest is at once a tribute to Tom and a proof of the villain's myopia. "As for any lucrative motives, he imagined they would sway very little with so silly a fellow" (273). But it is Blifil himself who is the silly son of a silly father, digging pits for others and falling into them himself. Because his sole aim is to cheat others, he assumes that everyone is out to cheat him, and this is a blunder that brings about his own downfall.

Evil is stupid; when the heart is corrupted, the head is unsound. The bad man is a bad judge, as Blifil's presumptuous, conceited court-ship of Sophia so amply demonstrates; he "saw no bar to his success with Sophia," while all the time the girl loathes him (274). Fielding puzzled over the mystery that men might go to heaven with half the pains it costs them to go to hell (*JW*, 220), and Blifil is his prime example of this assiduous, perverted industry. At the end he can be left to marry his widow and plan his parliamentary career, a comic figure, too much of a fool to be a menace. His very lies, even when successful, are for Fielding a species of folly, a self-deception even more than a deception of others; they deceive Allworthy for a time, God never. God alone, as Milton points out in *Paradise Lost,* can defend us from hypocrites.[19] It is the crucial single difference between Fielding and Orwell. O'Brien and Winston, atheists both, agree that God cannot check Big Brother, for he does not exist—there is only one God and O'Brien is his prophet. But, for Fielding, even the successful sinner is a fool, because God exists, and *he* cannot be hoodwinked. No God, no comedy. Many Christians have argued for God as the guarantor of morality (without God everything is permitted). Field-ing's variant is to propose God as the surety of comedy, sponsor of the triumph of the goodwill, final underwriter of the comic contract in *Tom Jones.*

Confusion arises from our assumption that humanism and reli-gion are hostile to each other; for Fielding, on the contrary, they are allies, and, consequently, the relationship between secular and sacred is in him more complex than we may be prepared to allow. As a co-median, Fielding is explicitly committed to the happy ending: "Had we been of the tragic complexion" (777); but this is clearly a contrary-to-fact conditional—the real world of woe is to be superimposed upon a comic grid. And, taxing though the enterprise be, we sense behind the bogus defeatism ("a task indeed so hard that we do not undertake to execute it") the delight of the artist confronting the fascination of the difficult and confident of his power to solve the problem (777).

The artist proclaims the exactingness of the project, not as an advance excuse for failure, but as a prelude to success: in three days I shall rebuild this temple. The means may still be obscure but the conclusion is assured. "We almost despair of bringing him to any good"; the significant, the giveaway, word is "almost"; the alert reader will not rush out to book his seat at Tyburn; Tom is not for hanging.

But as a novelist, working in the new form that has said goodbye to God, farewell to the supernatural, Fielding must contrive his happy ending without the celestial assistance or machinery so readily available to the writer of romance or epic. Tom must be saved by natural means or not at all. In the age of Hume there can be no miracles; the novelist must rescue Tom, not the hagiographer. The narrator, contrasting his straitened condition with that of the privileged ancients, Arabians and Persians, all of whom had an easy recourse to supernatural aid, describes himself as "a poor circumscribed modern" (778); but this is disingenuous. Despite Lukács, there is, in this novelist at least, no sense of abandonment or anguish at God's desertion but rather a *superbia*, a pride in the ability of the autonomous artist to resolve his difficulties without the invocation of some deus ex machina. No parting of the Red Sea is required; Tom will be saved by Fielding, not by God.

But if Fielding as artist is God's rival, it is in a spirit of reverent imitation, not of belligerent rejection. Man, too, is a creator, is called on by God to be a creator, to join with him in the as yet uncompleted creation of the world, but as colleague, not competitor. Moreover, this later, secondary creation finds its inspiration in, could not *be*, without the primal creation of Genesis. The artist supplements but does not supplant the original maker. Behind Fielding's humanism is the reinforcement of religion, however removed. It would be a mistake to believe that Fielding merely doffs his cap to religion in the token gesture of a polite Augustan gentleman; the heavenly backdrop, the guarantees of God, are no mere cardboard expedient, painted and insubstantial, to a tale exclusively rooted in earth. Fielding's humanism meshes easily and naturally with religion, forever prepared to draw on it in time of need.

The quotation from Terence endorsing humanism must not be

misinterpreted as hostility to religion, because what people believe, including their faith in a controlling Providence, also belongs to the natural world (724); and Fielding's good characters are all convinced that this world is finally in God's hands. "Good Heaven! by what wonderful means is the blackest and deepest villainy sometimes discovered!" (838). Allworthy's only error here is to say "sometimes" rather than "always." The means, however striking, are strictly secular, but God employs his earthly instruments to produce the felicitous outcome. "I discovered his name by a very odd accident" (838). Dowling's attempt to conceal his identity is futile, though it is the worldly Partridge, not an angel from heaven, who recognizes him. But far from being odd or accidental, it confirms the underlying providential assurance that the wicked will be detected, that their sins will find them out, that the snares they set for others will be their own undoing. Allworthy visits old Nightingale just when Black George is present; it is "an accident . . . of a very extraordinary kind, one indeed of those strange chances, whence very good and grave men have concluded that Providence often interposes in the discovery of the most secret villainy, in order to caution men from quitting the paths of honesty, however warily they tread in those of vice" (819). There is, clearly, pattern here rather than mere coincidence. The wicked are warned: just when they think themselves secure, the pit yawns for them. It is the converse of the situation in *Nineteen Eighty-four:* there the deluded rebel, safe, as he thinks, in his room-haven, is all the time in the power of the Thought Police—good is helpless, evil omnipotent. In *Tom Jones* the rascals are doomed to detection, for God is both supreme and good. What seems like sheer accident is really providential design.

Allworthy laments the radiation of evil: "How much beyond our designs are the effects of wickedness sometimes carried!" (833). Tom's initial offense in sleeping with Mrs. Waters has tragically escalated into unintentional incest. In fact, it has not. What the book demonstrates is not the power but the impotence of evil, the triumph of the *felix culpa,* as the wicked do their worst and succeed only in bringing forth good. It is, indeed, the converse that is blessedly true: it is goodness that has its unseen ramifications, its unpredictable ripples, its unpremeditated effects, which no one, including the deed's performer, could have foretold or foreseen. If the kingdom is pursued strenuously enough, all the other good things will follow: here is the basic Christianity of Fielding's art.

The importance of religion in providing the infrastructure for this comedy cannot be exaggerated. Sophia, attempting to convince her mistrustful aunt that she will never see Tom again, offers to receive the sacrament upon it (790). What would be the point of such an assurance if neither giver nor receiver took it seriously? What equivalent assurance could any heroine of the post-Christian era give? Allworthy warns both Western and Blifil in the gravest terms against forcing Sophia into a marriage she abhors, not simply because it is an act of oppression, at odds with natural justice and the law of England, but chiefly because it is impious, an offense against the law of heaven. It will ruin Sophia's life on earth, but, far worse, may lead to her eternal damnation (784–85). A tyrannical parent may be sending his daughter literally to hell, and for this he, too, will answer at the bar of heaven. The next world still matters, whether as threat or promise. One need only compare how Fielding's great inheritor, Dickens, handles an analogous situation in *Hard Times*. Gradgrind bears a grievous responsibility for Louisa's ruined life, but there is no hint of either's suffering being extended into the hereafter. It would be foolish to conclude that religion is unimportant for Fielding because he takes it for granted, for that is precisely the proof of how important it is. Old Nightingale is described as "a man of the world; that is to say, a man who directs his conduct in this world, as one who being fully persuaded there is no other, is resolved to make the best of this" (682–83). Evidently, for Fielding, it makes a difference to one's conduct (presumably for the better) if one believes in the world to come.

So crucial is this belief to Fielding that his attack on the optimists is not simply because what they teach is untrue (the good are not necessarily rewarded in this life), but because it is morally subversive; it undermines "one of the noblest arguments that reason alone can furnish for the belief of immortality" (696). Christianity tells us that heaven exists; reason tells us it *must* exist. Virtue *must* be rewarded, somewhere, sometime. It follows that because the good often fail in this world, there must be another world in which they always triumph. Reason supplements revelation. So essential is the idea of immortality to Fielding that the great optimist, temporarily and, as we shall see, inconsistently, becomes the scourge of the optimists when he sees their teaching as threatening this precious doctrine.

The importance of religion becomes more pronounced as the novel moves toward its climax. Square, in his letter of contrition, exalts Christianity above the noblest philosophy because it is the strongest promoter of the doctrine of immortality: "I never was much in earnest in this faith, till I was in earnest a Christian" (823). Allworthy warns Mrs. Waters to tell the truth about Tom's parentage by reminding her that "there is one from whom you can conceal nothing, and before whose tribunal falsehood will only aggravate your guilt" (835). We must wait for *Nineteen Eighty-four* to hear the same positive assertion concerning the futility of lying—O'Brien tells Winston how senseless it is to attempt to deceive Big Brother—but the surface similarity reveals how terrifyingly the world has changed, for Fielding's undeceivable God, unlike the idol of Oceania, is the friend of man and the stay of virtue.

On the negative side, the idiom and imagery of religion are recruited to define the villain's role and situation. Blifil is an eighteenth-century Faustus who has made his deal with the devil, and, as is the devil's way, he remains faithful to his friend "till their bargain expires" (829). (The novel's prohibition of the supernatural seems temporarily relaxed: the new fiction is off limits to God, but the devil still has rights of visitation.) Tom, in his transition from decent man to Christian hero, pleads for his enemy, and the basis of his appeal is that the despairing Blifil is unfit to die in his present situation, because his soul would go straight to hell; what Hamlet wants for Claudius is what Tom wants to avert for Blifil (860). Small wonder that Mrs. Miller should regard her hero as too good for this world; the Good Samaritan only saved a stranger—Tom strives to save the foe who has plotted his destruction.

Perhaps the strongest indication of religion's importance is the use of its terminology in situations where the purely secular, the affairs of this world, might be thought to prevail. Allworthy bids his servant to tell Blifil, "he knew him not" (859). It is a heightened, almost a biblical, language, evocative of the comminatory psalms, God turning his face away in anger from the sinner. The idioms of religion are applied quite naturally to the realm of personal relations and especially to love. For Tom, to possess Sophia would be the highest blessing of heaven, but Allworthy warns him that his case is "desperate" and Tom dolefully agrees: "I have sinned against her beyond all hopes of pardon." His "guilt" and "follies" are "irretrievable," and all of Allworthy's goodness cannot save him from "perdition" (855). It is the idiom of a damned soul rather than that of a disappointed lover. Just before the final reconciliation, Tom is still speaking a religious language, but it is now that of hope rather than despair, of salvation rather than damnation. He asks for mercy, not justice—like any sinner he knows that justice will condemn him (864)—and Sophia responds in like manner: "sincere repentence . . . will obtain the pardon of a sinner" (865). A courtship is conducted in the language of the confessional, with absolution sought and given. Finally, the novel ends with the assurance that "all were happy, but those the most, who had been most unhappy before" (870)—exactly in accord with the equity of the Christian promise that the recompense of heaven will be in proportion to the tribulations of earth.

Is it necessary to repeat that the optimism under discussion refers to Fielding's fiction and not to what he believed were the actual transactions of everyday life? True, in the legacy inherited by liberalism from Christianity is the idea of a secularized Providence: truth must prevail, good triumph, evil self-destruct. But in both creeds is an eschatological element, a vision of history come to perfection. No Christian or liberal would argue that the actual experience of life, the brute facts of existence, could be cited in triumphant vindication of this faith. If it were so, faith would be redundant, for faith is the substance of things hoped for, the evidence of things not seen. Fielding knew only too well that the world is unjust, that the innocent suffer and the guilty escape. But, however true of the world he surveyed, this is irrelevant to the world he created.

Within his art he verifies the promise shared by Christianity and liberalism alike that the good heart is sacrosanct, that whoever means well and strives manfully shall not be allowed to perish. In *Jonathan Wild* the nameless good magistrate ensures the happy ending through his commendable readiness to admit a mistake rather than connive at a miscarriage of justice. In Fielding's fiction there is always a good magistrate, if not literally among the dramatis personae, then in the person of the narrator himself—and he has the additional merit of being infallible. The fear of every good magistrate (that he may condemn an innocent man), the fear of every accused innocent (that he may be found guilty), are both averted. Justice is guaranteed now, and Providence is a pseudonym for Henry Fielding.

But God, in turn, is Fielding's guarantor. Facing certain condemnation for the killing of Fitzpatrick, Tom resigns all hope in earthly help, but affirms his "reliance on a Throne still greatly superior; which will, I am certain, afford me all the protection I merit" (808). This is no mere rhetorical flourish—men about to be hanged mean what they say. "I hope the Divine Goodness will one day suffer my honour to be cleared, and that the words of a dying man at least, will be believed, so far as to justify his character" (808). It is the prayer that Winston Smith, in parallel circumstances, cannot utter, the posthumous vindication that O'Brien so decisively denies. But it is, in the event, irrelevant, however consoling, because in Fielding's fictional world we need not attend eternity to obtain justice.

Fielding incarnates in a fiction the opening of the Lord's Prayer: thy will be done on earth as it is in heaven. Tom will not be hanged or press-ganged, nor Blifil scheme his way into Allworthy's fortune and Sophia's bed. That such injustices may well happen in life makes Fielding the more determined that they shall not happen in his art—in this domain, too, the Father's will is accomplished. To put it in terms of Fielding's other profession, the fact that wrong verdicts and miscarriages of justice are unavoidable in the courts of men stiffens Fielding's resolve that they shall not occur in the court of his fiction. Against our legal fiction, our hypocrisy, that the man found guilty must be guilty, Fielding musters the good, redeeming fictions of art, deliberately (for some critics, shamelessly) parading the artifice of his novelistic strategies of salvation. Ford Madox Ford, who insists that the novelist should adopt a strategy of concealment, hiding the secrets of his art from profane eyes, was outraged at what for him was Fielding's betrayal—a fellow-mason brazenly revealing the secrets of the craft to outsiders (Rawson, 346–47)—but it is precisely Fielding's delight in the craft that makes him so eager to communicate the novel's gospel, the good news of art, to all and sundry: those that have ears to hear, let them hear. Ford thinks that the novel ought to simulate the reality of life; Fielding, believing that this alleged "reality" is itself a fiction, a hypocrisy, calls attention to this through the deliberate artifice of his own tale.

Fielding is the magistrate-novelist, recruiting the genius of the second vocation to remedy the shortcomings of the first. To this end he imports the assurances of heaven to resolve the predicaments of earth, as his description of conscience so strikingly shows. He likens it to the Lord High Chancellor in his court, "where it presides, governs, directs, judges, acquits, and condemns according to merit and justice; with a knowledge which nothing escapes, a penetration which nothing can deceive, and an integrity which nothing can corrupt" (168). This, apparently legal, is really theological; it describes God, not the Lord High Chancellor, for such judicial perfection is to be found only in the court of heaven. Every Christian must believe that one day justice shall be done; Fielding in his art declares that the day is now.

This is why the narrator is ultimately the most important character in the work, superintendent of the comic warranty. Tom's good fortune is to have Fielding as his progenitor, literary equivalent of the loving Father of Christian doxology. Nowhere else in secular literature is the reader so sharply conscious of the author as pervasively benevolent deity, as the novel's god, forever overseeing and guiding the action. The good characters are his instruments but, exactly as in the Christian scheme, could not of themselves achieve the comic resolution. Complementing the goodwill of the hero is the fine intelligence of the narrator: *mens sana in corpore sano;* as Henry James judiciously notes, Tom contributes the robust body, the narrator the discriminating mind (Rawson, 328). Despite being a good man,

Allworthy goes consistently wrong; his cry of self-reproach near the close alerts us to the tragedy that must surely have occurred had the omniscient, benevolent narrator, the book's guardian, not been at his post.

The easy, confident tone of the narrator can come from only one of two things: fatuous complacency or comic control; either the speaker is a fool or master of the game. We need not read far to discover the answer, and the confidence is contagious; this fiction is so clearly ensured against calamity, in tiny detail as in total structure. Infallibility unites with generosity to create a world in which merit and reward are perfectly matched. Comedy is always concerned with revelation, with stripping and unmasking, with making the hoarded secret public property; identity is manifested in community, human beings revealed for what they truly are in terms of their relations to each other.

Comedy is a social product, a gregarious enterprise. It follows that the characters of comedy are under no artistic obligation to change, because they exist not to develop but to be undraped in the presence of their peers: Square in Molly's room, the naked truth behind the displaced rug, Gulliver shivering stripped in the Yahoo lineup, his real identity mortifyingly exposed. (This basic truth about comedy has, nevertheless, not saved Fielding from being censured because his characters do not develop; inappropriate criteria are frequently employed in decrying Fielding's work.) No change has occurred, save in perception; things are just as they always were, except that we no longer see through a glass darkly. Tom, mistaken for a scamp, is shown as the good man he always was; Blifil, always a rogue, is at last unmasked. Private and public coalesce.

Comedy is an epiphany and the publicity of the disclosure is the salient fact. Herein lies the difference, theologically speaking, between the individual judgment after death, the private confrontation of Creator and creature, and the Last Judgment when the souls of all who have lived are gathered to be communally, publicly assigned the kind of eternity each has merited. Hence the essentially *comic* appeal of the Last Judgment during the era of Western faith as the moment of final reckoning: all shall be made known, every dark corner illuminated, all wrongs righted, all hitherto slippery malefactors caught, all hitherto neglected deservers rewarded, an exact correlation between performance and assessment achieved—at long last, justice, that *ignis fatuus* of earth, shall be detained in heaven.

Fielding might be praised in ethics as Pope praises Newton in physics, as a light bearer. There are no dark corners in Fielding, save for those, like the noisome mind of Blifil, he categorically declines to enter, and here he challenges us to fault this self-restraint (157, also 861). Is it not enough to see and smell the filth, must you wade through it too before you credit its existence? Some modern critics patronize Fielding because his world is *too* bright, or blame him for refusing to penetrate the chthonian depths he admits are there.[20] Such criticisms are really a complaint that he is not another kind of artist, because, first, the brightness is that of the comic epiphany, and, second, Fielding has revealed enough of Blifil for judgment to be made; to provide more filth would be excessive, to demand it, perverse.

It should be, and is certainly meant to be, a reassurance to find ourselves the jurors of such a judge. Despite the Gospel injunction, it is impossible to live in the world and renounce judgment. We have to judge, despite knowing that there is no infallible court or magistrate, no jury immune from misdirection. Our best hope is that mistakes should at least be corrigible. Crucial in the campaign to abolish the death penalty was the admission that innocent men have been hanged. Have fallible men the right to make irreparable mistakes? A hanged man is guilty forever; an Alps of subsequent contrary evidence cannot revoke this brutal fact. As the faith that the condemned Tom has in the next world wanes, the need to prevent irrevocable blunders in this one becomes the more exigent. Perhaps any Last Judgment is indefensible; one pronounced by a creature conscious of fallibility seems outrageous. Fielding liberates us from our cognitive misgivings by conferring, within his fiction, the gift of infallibility on mistake-prone men; his readers join him on a bench secured against error.

Yet the idea of a Last Judgment may chill as well as console. What if the judge awaiting us is someone like Swift's terrible joker in "The Day of Judgement," implacable, sadistic? Here is the second source of

Fielding's appeal: *his* last judgment will frighten only the incorrigibly vicious. Swift's satire, at its most characteristic, teeters on the brink of explosive exasperation, Jehovah about to pulverize a besotted people. Swift will not go on prescribing a dose for the dead; Gulliver tells Cousin Sympson that Yahoo reform is a delusion he has abandoned forever.[21] Only a fatuous reader of Swift will dream himself exempt from the general incrimination. This is a hanging judge, harsh and unforgiving.

Fiat justitia et pereat mundus: the sentiment, so thoroughly at home in Swift, is unthinkable in Fielding. He loves the world too much to sacrifice it to any abstraction, however exalted; even the beloved Aeschylus burns in the grate until Adams first makes sure that no harm has come to Fanny (*JA,* 156–57). Life always comes first. A woman may very reasonably object to a naked man in a coach, but not when excluding him means death or injury; then such scruples must be exposed for the hypocrisies they are, for modesty, like Aeschylus, does not count when life is at risk (*JA,* 64). It is the Pharisee who sets law above life, the Sabbath above man. The court over which Fielding presides is marked by tolerance, even indulgence; those condemned there will be pressed to find exoneration anywhere.

Lady Mary is really asking Fielding to be Richardson when she complains that his young lovers are not prudent and forethoughtful, replicas of Pamela. Fielding, however, had not written *Shamela* in order to end up celebrating what he had ridiculed. Yet the irony is that all Fielding's books might equally bear the subtitle of *Virtue Rewarded.* Richardson wrote *Clarissa* whose heroine must await her reward in eternity; nowhere in Fielding does virtue fail to reap its reward in this world. The quarrel with Richardson is over means, not ends. Pamela is a careerist, Tom the happy-go-lucky beneficiary of his own and his creator's good heart, but each is a success story. In both novels, Providence, moving in its own mysterious ways, seeks out and blesses the virtuous, though Pamela, as attentive pupil, meets her benefactor halfway. The difference is not that one is rewarded and the other not, nor is it even in the kind of reward (who will distinguish between the marital bliss of Tom and Pamela?); rather it is that each is rewarded by very different moralists employing radically opposed criteria. Fielding contemptuously denies that Pamela is a good woman; she is merely a shrewd accountant, and that, if anything, ranks her with Blifil rather than with Tom. Richardson, in retaliation, sees Tom as a drunken libertine, in Lady Mary's phrase, "a sorry scoundrel," who is reprieved from his just deserts by his complaisant creator-accomplice. Sophia, Fielding's ideal woman, modeled upon his beloved dead wife, is prudishly dismissed by Richardson as an indiscreet baggage who goes traipsing about the countryside in pursuit of a rascal (Rawson, 107), though Fielding specifically warns against seeing her in this light (502). The gods of the one writer are the demons of the other; what the one reveres the other reviles.

But neither writer ascetically restricts virtue to its own reward. Fielding, despite ridiculing the belief that happiness always accompanies virtue in this world, is even more determined than his rival to reward virtue here and now, because his comedy is geocentric. Richardson can eschew earthly happiness because he holds the prize of heaven in reserve for Clarissa, but Fielding's fiction shows no great interest in the paradise to come; he knows no greater earthly felicity than marriage to a woman like Sophia, and the decisiveness of his expression reveals that he has not been speculating as to what may happen afterward. Empson correctly discovers Fielding's "secret" in his celebration of this world (Rawson, 503)—Tom's pleasure with Mrs. Waters, though inferior to that with Sophia, is a real value, certainly not in itself cause for a hair shirt—but it is surely a very ill-kept secret to any attentive reader of Fielding. In *Joseph Andrews* punch is preferable to prayers, shirts are more serviceable than sermons, and the book's moment of supreme joy is when the drowned child is restored to life; all the copybook maxims of religious consolation are dross in comparison with the living human being (*JA*, 75, 101, 290–91). *This* Abraham, unlike Kierkegaard's ecstatic knight of faith, rebels against his son's sacrifice and will not be comforted by the promise of reunion in heaven. Fielding celebrates the life we have. Joseph may compare himself to the tragic hero of *The London Merchant* (*JA*, 50), Tom miscast himself as Oedipus (815), Sophia steel herself, like

Chaucer's Virginia, for death before dishonor (320), but Fielding is not auditioning for these roles. Unlike Richardson in *Clarissa,* he will not rely on heaven to recompense virtue, but supplies without fail the terrestrial happy ending. "Secret" is a curious word to apply to something so glaringly obvious.

It does, however, make his attack on the optimists more puzzling: "There are a set of religious, or rather moral writers, who teach that virtue is the certain road to happiness, and vice to misery, in this world. A very wholesome and comfortable doctrine, and to which we have but one objection, namely, that it is not true" (695). One recalls Hardy's onslaught on Wordsworthian optimism in *Tess of the d'Urbervilles.*[22] But Hardy consistently matches his tale to his doctrine: If you mean to demolish the fiction that goodness always triumphs in this world, how better to do it than through the tragic legend of the betrayed maiden, who, unlike Tom Jones, does end up on the gallows? The appropriate response to shallow optimism is tragedy; when the world is misrepresented through rose-colored glasses, darker lenses must be prescribed. Hardy, outrageously for some readers, conspires with coincidence to contrive Tess's destruction. Fielding, curiously for a man who has just blasted the optimists, uses coincidence in an equally obtrusive way to bring about the happy ending; coincidence is really the servant of Providence. For Hardy there is no justice, here or anywhere else: "The President of the Immortals had finished his sport with Tess." For Fielding there is always justice, frequently in the world, unfailingly in his fiction—an intriguing stance for the scourge of the optimists. In *Tom Jones* he ridicules a particular set of writers and then joins their company.

This is doubly ironic in that a major theme in Fielding is the comic discrepancy between deed and word, profession and practice. His insistence that deeds are a more reliable testimony than words makes it the more piquant to detect the same divergence in himself. The rebuttal of the Butlerian view that virtue must procure happiness in this world is not, of course, an argument for vice; Fielding wants men to continue virtuous but to abandon the pretense that they must profit thereby; virtue is its own reward and often its only one.

But if this is what he says, his books tell a different story. The good characters can be careless of their interests in texts whose author is so vigilantly safeguarding them. Hardy says that Wordsworth is wrong and tries to show it; Fielding derides optimism and creates a masterpiece of optimistic comedy. All his books, including his most somber production, *Amelia*, in which the temptation to despond is at its greatest, are triumphs of juridical optimism. The happy ending of *Amelia* strikes many readers almost as a violation, and there is, unquestionably, something especially contrived about this finale, reminiscent of a deus ex machina or the sensational denouements of old Hollywood B-movie courtroom dramas. Beside the wish fulfillment of *Amelia, Pamela* seems like sober realism. But if the means surprise, the end surely does not. Who, knowing Fielding, expects tragedy? How could a good magistrate like Fielding allow his favored characters to come to grief? Unite the magistrate's benevolence with the comedian's genius and the happy ending is the only predictable outcome.

Trust the tale; for all his talk of virtue being its own reward, Fielding strives to make Tom happy. In *Amelia*, Dr. Harrison expresses the orthodox sentiments of Christian stoicism: "A true Christian can never be disappointed if he doth not receive his reward in this world; the labourer might as well complain that he is not paid his hire in the middle of the day" (*A*, 396). Doubtless, Fielding the Christian agrees: it is Fielding the novelist who wants payment now. There is no postponement of wages in *Tom Jones*, no moratorium while earthly injustice awaits heaven's reversal. Tom receives his wages in the middle of the day, that is, in the present world. A wageless world, barren of justice, is a nightmare beyond Fielding's consent. Bertolt Brecht in *The Threepenny Opera* erupts in irritated irony at the convention of happy-ever-after: "So the whole thing has a happy ending! How calm and peaceful would our life be always if a messenger came from the king whenever we wanted!"[23] Fielding in his fiction is the king's messenger and his readers can always count on a royal pardon or a timely reprieve. There is, finally, no contradiction between his ridicule of the optimists and the optimism of his own work: they foolishly guarantee happiness in life; Fielding guarantees it only in his fiction. Kafka is the place to go if we want to read about unattainable justice and frustrated plaintiffs. In Fielding, by contrast, we witness the comedy of justice—his trial is always an exoneration and his castle always a refuge. That is why his work is the perfect secular embodiment of the good news that Christianity brings.

Conclusion

There is much that we must unlearn before we can bring to a reading of *Tom Jones* the proper, the necessary expectations. We must discard a whole set of prejudices and preconceptions that we parade as our wisdom when they merely signal our parochialism. Certain assumptions impede appropriate contact with the text. We take it for granted that religion and humanism are incompatible, and that a vote for earth is a rebuff to heaven; we easily invoke *the* tradition of the novel (usually meaning Richardsonian), when we are, at most, entitled to speak of *a* tradition, one among several, each equally valid; we uncritically absorb Arnold's dictum that seriousness means solemnity, and that comedy is the lesser form.

Fielding disagrees. Tom is, simultaneously, the champion of man against the misanthropic recluse, and the true Christian of his claim to the revenge-inciting lieutenant (431–32, 349); there is no irreconcilability. Our partisanship for a certain kind of novel leads us into the cardinal error of judging one style by criteria appropriate to another, and so we too easily elect Richardson above Fielding. But here, too, there is another view based on another aesthetic preference. Whatever turmoil the artist is in, his job is not to infect us with the turmoil. At least, not necessarily. Richardson labors to immerse us in the turmoil; the aim is contagion, complicity. We are to be taken inside Lovelace, made to feel as he does, momentarily become him, however unpleasant the experience, for, as Walter Pater says, not the fruit of experience but experience itself is the end.[1] For Fielding, such abandon is both dangerous and decadent, and so he keeps the turmoil at a distance;

Blifil's mind is a no-go area, strictly off limits. Inside the stream of consciousness, we drift with the stream, but Fielding prefers us to stand safely on shore, assessing, not surrendering to, the experience; for it is the fruit of experience that matters. The triumph of Fielding's art is that we know Blifil without having to take up residence within that unwholesome skull; character is comprehended from without, not identified from within.

Coleridge's remark that Richardson is *only* interesting implies that Fielding has the edge in wisdom,[2] and it is Richardson's admirer who concedes that his hero's presentational realism had to be complemented by Fielding's wisdom of assessment, his syntax of judgment, if the new genre was to realize its full potential.[3] Consciousness can become a tedium—we have been imprisoned in too many minds since Stephen Dedalus and Clarissa Dalloway, and we long to escape to the liberation of a detached, objective view. Our wish is no longer to feel with Sartre's Roquentin or Camus's Meursault, but to understand how and why such strange mentalities are bred. An answering art demands a critique, not a representation, detachment, not involvement; when you are too close, you cannot see, when you are a player, you cannot be a judge. It is such an art that Fielding solicits in his prayer to genius: "Teach me . . . to know mankind better than they know themselves" (608). How can you be at once the judge of Alceste and his second self? How can you detect self-deception if you identify with the self that deceives? The intimate involvement with character that Richardson nurtures will hinder rather than promote the knowledge that Fielding seeks.

Just as misplaced is our prejudice against comedy as somehow conveying a lesser truth or even a falsification. Dissatisfaction with Fielding sometimes stems from an aversion to comedy as something no higher than a pleasant way of passing time. Comedy seems to some a deception, a fabrication, in the sense that there is nothing out there, in bleak reality, that answers to it. There is no tone of complaint in Fielding, and, for us, not to speak in such a tone is to be insensitive and crass. We have seen through life for the shameful hoax it is; we prefer chaos to deception, and we are rather proud of ourselves for doing so. It is difficult to forgive Fielding's optimism, especially when our own knowledge of life has been so brutally, painfully earned. Fielding has already anticipated and rejected such a view: "surely a man may speak truth with a smiling countenance" (507). Must the evangelist be po-faced? Cannot the truth be happy?

And so in telling his story of the "natural" child with the commonplace name, the everyday hero of his comic epic, modestly rivaling in the variety of his allotted roles Homer's complete man, Ulysses, Fielding becomes a blithe evangelist, communicating the good news about life. Contemplating Tom as orphan, lover, supplicant for justice, truth-seeker, adventurer, Fielding brings glad reassurance concerning each of these destinies, and it is, for many moderns, too good to be true.

This orphan will come home to be reunited with his spiritual father, so unlike the hunted protagonist of Faulkner's *Light in August*, homeless forever, orphaned eternally, dying his bloody death still not knowing, fated never to know, who he is. This lover is as fortunate as Bassanio, winning both golden girl and golden mountain, in sharp contrast to Julien Sorel or Gatsby or even Pip, whose fairy-gold disappears overnight, who gets, after many years, not the golden girl but the chastened woman, and even that only because Dickens relented. This supplicant for justice, so removed from the bewildered plaintiff of *The Trial*, will receive in the end not merely justice but, better still, mercy.

This truth-seeker—the term is misleading because, in Fielding, truth comes to the hero as a free gift, the bounty of Providence, without his striving after it—will discover truth, and, unlike Oedipus, it will be, as Christianity promises, a truth that sets him free. Finally, this adventurer, so different from that long succession of his peers from Don Quixote to Emma Bovary and Isabel Archer and on to Kafka's land surveyor, abortive adventurers all, each in his or her situation of tragic entrapment, with longings never to be placated in a world not up to their dreams, will bring *his* quest to completely happy fulfillment, in which no jot of satisfaction is lacking, no iota of desire left unassuaged.

Tom Jones is a book in which dreams are realized and promises kept. What, for a modern reader, could be more startling than that?

Notes and References

1. The Rivalries of Art

1. Frank Kermode in *The Novel Today: Contemporary Writers on Modern Fiction*, ed. Malcolm Bradbury (Glasgow: Fontana-Collins, 1977), 112.

2. Lady Mary Wortley Montague in *Henry Fielding: A Critical Anthology*, ed. Claude Rawson (Harmondsworth, Middlesex: Penguin, 1973), 132–33 (hereafter cited in the text as Rawson).

3. *Henry Fielding: The Critical Heritage*, ed. Ronald Paulson and Thomas Lockwood (London: Routledge and Kegan Paul; New York: Barnes and Noble, 1969), 175.

4. Maynard Mack in *Literature Criticism from 1400 to 1800*, vol. 1, ed. Dennis Poupard and Mark W. Scott (Detroit: Gale Research Company, 1984), 230–31; hereafter cited in the text as *Lit. Crit.*

5. Charlotte Brontë, *Jane Eyre*, ed. Q. D. Leavis (Harmondsworth, Middlesex: Penguin, 1966), 344.

6. F. R. Leavis, *The Great Tradition: George Eliot, Henry James, Joseph Conrad* (Harmondsworth, Middlesex: Penguin, 1972), 12.

2. The Importance of the Work

1. E. M. Forster, *Abinger Harvest* (London: Edward Arnold, 1942), 139.

2. Leavis, *The Great Tradition*, 11.

3. Lionel Trilling, *Sincerity and Authenticity* (London: Oxford University Press, 1974), 1.

4. Patrick Reilly, *The Literature of Guilt: From "Gulliver" to Golding* (London: Macmillan; Ames: University of Iowa Press, 1988), 15–20.

5. *Jonathan Wild*, ed. David Nokes (Harmondsworth, Middlesex: Penguin, 1982), 30; hereafter cited in the text as *JW*.

6. *Amelia*, ed. David Blewett (Harmondsworth, Middlesex: Penguin, 1987), 380–82; hereafter cited in the text as *A*.

7. See also Fielding's quotation from "my beloved Author, Dr. Barrow": "A man may be virtuously voluptuous, and a laudable epicure by doing much good," in *The Covent-Garden Journal and A Plan of the Universal Register-Office*, ed. Bertrand A. Goldgar (Oxford: Clarendon Press, 1988), 186.

8. Samuel Johnson, "The Rambler," no. 4, 31 March 1750, in *Selected Writings*, ed. Patrick Cruttwell (Harmondsworth, Middlesex: Penguin, 1968), 151.

3. Critical Reception

1. See Samuel Johnson, in *Henry Fielding: Tom Jones, A Casebook*, ed. Neil Compton (London: Macmillan, 1970), 30–32; hereafter cited in the text as Compton.

2. Denis Diderot, "Éloge de Richardson," *Oeuvres complètes*, vol. 5 (Paris: Garnier Frères, 1875), 216.

3. See Samuel Taylor Coleridge, in Compton, 32–35.

4. Henry James, in Compton, 58–59, and, for the two-plot theory, Wayne C. Booth, *The Rhetoric of Fiction* (Chicago: University of Chicago Press, 1961), 216–18.

5. Aldous Huxley, "Tragedy and the Whole Truth," in *Tragedy: Developments in Criticism, a Casebook*, ed. R. P. Draper (London and Basingstroke: Macmillan, 1980), 153.

6. Samuel Johnson, in Compton, p. 31.

7. William Hazlitt, in Compton, p. 41.

8. F. R. Leavis, *The Great Tradition*, p. 12.

9. See Booth, *The Rhetoric of Fiction*, p. 217.

10. See Robert Alter, *Fielding and the Nature of the Novel* (Cambridge, Mass.: Harvard University Press, 1968), pp. 138–39.

4. Fighting the Pharisees

1. William Hazlitt, "Characteristics," in *The Collected Works of William Hazlitt*, vol. 2, ed. A. R. Waller and Arnold Glover (London: J. M. Dent and Co., 1902), 392.

2. For instance, Hans Küng, in *On Being a Christian*, trans. Edward Quinn (Glasgow: Collins, Fount Paperbacks, 1978), 202–11.

3. *Joseph Andrews*, ed. R. F. Brissenden (Harmondsworth, Middlesex: Penguin, 1977), 93; hereafter cited in the text as *JA*.

4. By John Preston, *The Created Self: The Reader's Role in Eighteenth-Century Fiction* (London: Heinemann, 1970), 114–32.

5. *The Complete Poems and Plays of T.S. Eliot* (London and Boston: Faber and Faber, 1969), 258.

6. Franz Kafka, *The Trial*, trans. Willa and Edwin Muir (Harmondsworth, Middlesex: Penguin, 1953), 97.

7. Quoted in Roland Stromberg, *Religious Liberalism in Eighteenth-Century England* (Oxford: Oxford University Press, 1954), 144 (note).

8. In Compton, 34–35.

9. Edmund Burke, *Reflections on the Revolution in France*, ed. Conor Cruise O'Brien (Harmondsworth, Middlesex: Penguin, 1969), 200.

10. John Milton, "Areopagitica," in *Selected Prose*, ed. C. A. Patrides (Harmondsworth, Middlesex: Penguin, 1974), 212–13.

11. Lord Clive quoted by Thomas Babington Macaulay, in *Lord Clive*, with introduction and notes by K. Deighton (London: Macmillan; New York: St. Martin's Press, 1960), 84.

12. *The Prose Works of Jonathan Swift*, vol. 1, ed. Herbert Davis (Oxford: Basil Blackwell, 1939), 190.

13. A. E. Dyson, *The Crazy Fabric: Essays in Irony* (London: Macmillan; New York: St. Martin's Press, 1965), 14–32.

14. Blaise Pascal, *Pensées*, trans. A. J. Krailsheimer (Harmondsworth, Middlesex: Penguin, 1966), 70–71.

15. Jane Austen, *Emma*, ed. Ronald Blythe (Harmondsworth, Middlesex: Penguin, 1966), 418.

16. Bernard Mandeville, *The Fable of the Bees*, ed. Philip Harth (Harmondsworth, Middlesex: Penguin, 1989), 88–91.

17. Dante Alighieri, *Divine Comedy*, "Paradise," 3, line 85.

5. Judging the Jurors

1. *Gulliver's Travels*, ed. Peter Dixon and John Chalker with an introduction by Michael Foot (Harmondsworth, Middlesex: Penguin, 1967), 340.

2. See *The Poems of Jonathan Swift*, vol. 2, ed. Harold Williams (Oxford, Clarendon Press, 1963–65), 579.

3. Scott, in Compton, p. 39.

4. Milan Kundera, *The Art of the Novel*, trans. Linda Asher (London and Boston: Faber and Faber, 1988), 6.

5. G. M. Hopkins, *A Selection of his Poems and Prose*, ed. W. H. Gardner (Harmondsworth, Middlesex: Penguin, 1953), 51.

6. Preston, *The Created Self*, 1–7.

7. Sigmund Freud, quoted in Bruno Bettelheim, *Freud and Man's Soul* (London: Flamingo, Fontana Paperbacks, 1985), 37.

8. See George Sherburn, "Fielding's Social Outlook," in *Eighteenth Century English Literature: Modern Essays in Criticism*, ed. James L. Clifford (New York: Galaxy, Oxford University Press, 1959), 251–72.

9. *The Complete Works of Geoffrey Chaucer*, ed. F. N. Robinson (London: Oxford University Press, 1957), 29.

10. See *The Works of Henry Fielding*, vol. 4, ed. James P. Browne (London: Bickers and Son, H. Sotheran and Co., 1871), 372.

11. *The Prose Works of Jonathan Swift*, 1:79–80.

12. Ibid., 9:73.

13. Ibid., 245.

14. Book 9, line 644.

15. Preston, *The Created Self*, 98, 107, 110–11.

16. Herman Melville, *The Confidence Man: His Masquerade* (New York: Signet Classics, New American Library, 1964), 40.

17. *Othello* 5.2.298–99.

18. See Carlos Fuentes, *Myself with Others: Selected Essays* (London: Picador, Pan Books, 1989), 52–71.

19. Kundera, *The Art of the Novel*, 6, 18.

6. Christening the Comedy

1. Pascal, *Pensées*, 59.

2. Fyodor Dostoyevski, *The Diary of a Writer*, vol. 2, trans. Boris Brasol (London: Cassell and Co., 1949), 836.

3. Irvin Ehrenpreis, *Fielding: Tom Jones* (London: Edward Arnold, 1964), 7.

4. Mary Poovey, "Journey from this World to the Next: The Providential Promise in *Clarissa* and *Tom Jones*," in *Eighteenth-Century British Fiction*, ed. Harold Bloom (New York, New Haven, Philadelphia: Chelsea House Publishers, 1988), 115.

5. Samuel Richardson, *Clarissa Harlowe; or, The History of a Young Lady*, vol. 7 (London: Chapman and Hall, 1902), 89.

6. Kundera, *The Art of the Novel*, 18.

7. Georg Lukács, *The Theory of the Novel* (London: Merlin Press, 1971), 88.

8. Kundera, *The Art of the Novel*, 6; Fuentes, *Myself with Others*, 57–58.

9. Miguel de Cervantes Saavedra, *The Adventures of Don Quixote*, trans. J. M. Cohen (Harmondsworth, Middlesex: Penguin, 1950), 641–42.

10. Fyodor Dostoyevski, *The Brothers Karamazov*, vol. 1, trans. David Magarshack (Harmondsworth, Middlesex: Penguin, 1958), 308–9.

11. Huxley, "Tragedy and the Whole Truth," 153.

12. *Revelations of Divine Love Recorded by Julian of Norwich*, ed. Grace Warrack (London: Methuen, 1901), 57; *The Tempest* 1.2.14–15.

13. *The Winter's Tale* 5.3.94–95.

14. Kundera, *The Art of the Novel*, 126, 136.

15. Georges Bernanos, *The Diary of a Country Priest*, trans. Pamela Morris (London: Fontana, 1977), 25.

16. Thackeray, in Compton, 45.

17. Aldous Huxley, *Island* (London: Triad-Grafton, Collins, 1986), 139.

18. Book 5, lines 735–37.

19. Book 3, lines 682–84.

20. See, for instance, Dorothy Van Ghent, in Compton, 75, 79–80.

21. *The Correspondence of Jonathan Swift*, vol. 3, ed. Harold Williams (Oxford: Clarendon Press, 1963), 501; *Gulliver's Travels*, 41.

22. Thomas Hardy, *Tess of the d'Urbervilles*, ed. David Skilton (Harmondsworth, Middlesex: Penguin, 1978), 61–62.

23. In *Gesammelte Werke* (Frankfurt am Main: Suhrkamp Verlag, 1967), vol. 2, 485: "So wendet alles sich am End zum Gluck. So leicht und friedlich wäre unser Leben, wenn die reitenden Boten des Königs immer kämen."

Conclusion

1. Walter Pater, *The Renaissance: Studies in Art and Poetry* (Glasgow: Fontana-Collins, 1961), 222.

2. Samuel Taylor Coleridge, quoted in Ian Watt, *The Rise of the Novel: Studies in Defoe, Richardson and Fielding* (London: Hogarth Press, 1987), 288.

3. Watt, *The Rise of the Novel*, 288–89.

Selected Bibliography

Primary Works

The Complete Works of Henry Fielding, Esq. Edited by William Ernest Henley. 16 vols., 1903; reprinted, New York: Barnes and Noble, 1967.

Amelia. Edited by Martin C. Battestin. Wesleyan Edition. Oxford: Clarendon Press, 1983.

An Apology for the Life of Mrs. Shamela Andrews. Introduction by Ian Watt. Augustan Reprint Society, no. 57. Los Angeles: William Andrews Clark Memorial Library, 1956.

The Author's Farce. Edited by Charles B. Woods. Regents Restoration Drama Series. Lincoln: University of Nebraska Press, 1966.

The Covent-Garden Journal. Edited by Gerard E. Jensen. 2 vols. New Haven: Yale University Press, 1915.

The Covent-Garden Tragedy. In *Burlesque Plays of the Eighteenth Century.* Edited by Simon Trussler. London: Oxford University Press, 1969.

The Grub-Street Opera. Edited by Edgar V. Roberts. Regents Restoration Drama Series. Lincoln: University of Nebraska Press, 1968.

The Historical Register for the Year 1736 and Eurydice Hiss'd. Edited by William W. Appleton. Regents Restoration Drama Series. Lincoln: University of Nebraska Press, 1967.

The History of Tom Jones. Edited by R. P. C. Mutter. Harmondsworth: Penguin, 1966.

The History of Tom Jones, a Foundling. Introduction and notes by Martin C. Battestin, edited by Fredson Bowers. 2 vols. Wesleyan Edition. Oxford: Clarendon Press, 1974.

The Jacobite's Journal and Related Writings. Edited by W. B. Coley. Wesleyan Edition. Oxford: Clarendon Press, 1975.

Jonathan Wild. Edited by David Nokes. Harmondsworth, Middlesex: Penguin, 1982.

Jonathan Wild and The Journal of a Voyage to Lisbon. Introduction by A. R. Humphreys, notes by Douglas Brooks. Everyman's Library. London: Dent, and New York: Dutton, 1973.

Joseph Andrews. Edited by Martin C. Battestin. Wesleyan Edition. Oxford: Clarendon Press, 1967.

A Journey from This World to the Next. Introduction by C. J. Rawson. Everyman's Library. London: Dent; New York: Dutton, 1973.

Miscellanies by Henry Fielding, Esq. Vol 1. Edited by Henry Knight Miller. Wesleyan Edition. Oxford: Clarendon Press, 1972.

Pasquin. Edited by O. M. Brack, Jr., William Kupersmith, and Curt Zimansky. Iowa City: University of Iowa Press, 1973.

Tom Thumb and the Tragedy of Tragedies. Edited by L. J. Morrissey. Fountainwell Drama Texts 14. Edinburgh: Oliver and Boyd; Berkeley and Los Angeles: University of California Press, 1970.

The True Patriot and The History of Our Times. Edited by Miriam Austin Locke. Tuscaloosa, Ala.: University of Alabama Press, 1964.

Secondary Works

Books

Alter, Robert. *Fielding and the Nature of the Novel.* Cambridge, Mass.: Harvard University Press, 1968. A stimulating and wide-ranging analysis of Fielding's art and artifice, proposing Fielding as the founder of the architectonic novel.

Banerji, H. K. *Henry Fielding: Playwright, Journalist, and Master of the Art of Fiction.* New York: Russell and Russell, 1962. Biography containing a critical survey of Fielding's lesser-known works (i.e., his dramas and journalism).

Battestin, Martin C. *The Moral Basis of Fielding's Art: A Study of Joseph Andrews.* Middletown, Conn.: Wesleyan University Press, 1959. Shows Fielding's indebtedness to latitudinarian Christianity, in particular to its doctrine of benevolence.

———. *The Providence of Wit: Aspects of Form in Augustan Literature and the Arts.* Oxford, Clarendon Press, 1974. Valuable chapters show that *Tom Jones* is constructed according to the Design Argument and that the novel's main theme is the achievement of wisdom.

———, ed. *Twentieth-Century Interpretations of "Tom Jones."* Englewood

Selected Bibliography

Cliffs, N.J.: Prentice-Hall, 1968. Useful collection of essays by Leavis, Watt, Empson, Crane, Booth, and others.

Blanchard, Frederic T. *Fielding the Novelist: A Study in Historical Criticism.* New Haven: Yale University Press, 1926. A thorough survey of critical attitudes to Fielding from his own time to 1925.

Booth, Wayne C. *The Rhetoric of Fiction.* Chicago: University of Chicago Press, 1961. Masterly treatment of problems of authorial intrusion and "point of view," with some stimulating pages on *Tom Jones.*

Butt, John. *Fielding.* Writers and their Work, No. 59. London: Longman, rev. ed., 1959. A good short guide to Fielding's career and works.

Cleary, Thomas R. *Henry Fielding: Political Writer.* Ontario: Wilfrid Laurier University Press, 1984. Attempts to provide a comprehensive study of the political aspects of Fielding's art by setting it against the foreign and domestic politics of his age.

Compton, Neil. *Henry Fielding: Tom Jones, A Casebook.* London and Basingstoke: Macmillan, 1970. A valuable collection of essays by modern critics, including Watt, Empson, Battestin, Paulson, Alter, and Preston.

Coventry, Francis. *An Essay on the New Species of Writing Founded by Mr. Fielding.* London: W. Owen, 1751; reprinted by University of California Press, 1962. One of the earliest appreciations of Fielding's contribution to the development of the modern novel; the "new species of writing" is characterized by a contemporary background, consistent character portrayal, and believable plots.

Cross, Wilbur S. *The History of Henry Fielding.* 3 vols. New Haven: Yale University Press, 1918. The standard biography, rectifying a number of misconceptions about Fielding and his works; discredits Murphy's image of Fielding as a "dissipated rake."

Ehrenpreis, Irvin. *Fielding: Tom Jones.* London: Edward Arnold, 1964. Excellent summary of modern critical views.

Golden, Morris. *Fielding's Moral Psychology.* Amherst: University of Massachusetts Press, 1966. An interesting discussion of "self-enclosure" in Fielding's fiction, emphasizing the moral importance of his work.

Goldgar, Bertrand A. *Walpole and the Wits: The Relation of Politics to Literature, 1722–42.* Lincoln and London: University of Nebraska Press, 1976. Charts Fielding's political affiliations, in a time of complex and confusing political relationships.

Harrison, Bernard. *Henry Fielding's "Tom Jones": The Novelist as Moral Philosopher.* London: Sussex University Press, 1975. Spirited defense of Fielding that sets him convincingly in the context of eighteenth-century philosophy.

Hatfield, Glenn W. *Henry Fielding and the Language of Irony.* Chicago: University of Chicago Press, 1968. Study of Fielding's struggle to maintain the integrity of the English language in the belief that the linguistic corruption of the age contributed to the undermining of society.

Hunter, J. Paul. *Occasional Form: Henry Fielding and the Chains of Circumstance*. Baltimore and London: Johns Hopkins University Press, 1975. Argues that the novels depend as much on contemporary issues as on traditional literary forms.

Hutchens, Eleanor N. *Irony in Tom Jones*. Tuscaloosa: University of Alabama Press, 1965. Discusses the theme of prudence as it is embodied in Fielding's "connotative irony."

Irwin, Michael. *Henry Fielding: The Tentative Realist*. Oxford: Clarendon Press, 1967. Shows Fielding as a didactic writer and moralist from the beginning of his literary career, as evidenced by his regular recurrence to specific social and ethical issues.

Johnson, Maurice. *Fielding's Art of Fiction: Eleven Essays on "Shamela," "Joseph Andrews," "Tom Jones," and "Amelia."* Philadelphia: University of Pennsylvania Press, 1961. Explicative essays on Fielding's literary devices.

Jones, B. M. *Henry Fielding: Novelist and Magistrate*. London: George Allen and Unwin, 1933. An early attempt to show the extent of Fielding's classical and legal knowledge and to call attention to his activity and success as a Bow Street magistrate.

Kalpakgian, Mitchell. *The Marvellous in Fielding's Novels*. Washington, D.C.: University Press of America, 1981. Relates Fielding's use of the marvelous to the eighteenth-century sublime.

Digeon, Aurélien. *The Novels of Fielding*. London: Routledge and Sons, 1925. A useful general study in which the author argues that there is a conflict in Fielding between magistrate and artist.

Dobson, Austin. *Fielding*. English Men of Letters Series, edited by John Morley. New York: Harper and Brothers, 1883. Presents the Victorian view of Fielding as a great novelist but a dissipated rake.

Dudden, F. Holmes. *Henry Fielding: His Life, Works, and Times*. 2 vols. Oxford: Clarendon Press, 1952; reprinted Hamden, Conn.: Archon Books, 1966. Extensive biography containing discussions of Fielding's works and their historical backgrounds.

Levine, George R. *Henry Fielding and the Dry Mock: A Study of the Techniques of Irony in His Early Works*. The Hague and Paris: Mouton, 1967. Examines in detail an aspect of the comic method of "one of the great literary craftsmen of the 18th century."

Lynch, James J. *Henry Fielding and the Heliodoran Novel: Romance, Epic and Fielding's New Province of Writing*. London and Toronto: Associated University Presses, 1986. Argues that a journey of two lovers, culminating in a marriage, had become the dominant structure for serious romance, and that Fielding's major fictions are modifications of this structure.

Miller, Henry Knight. *Essays on Fielding's Miscellanies: A Commentary on Volume One.* Princeton N.J.: Princeton University Press, 1961. Far more important and central than the title suggests; major commentary on Fielding's minor writings, with an excellent index.

————. *Henry Fielding's "Tom Jones" and the Romance Tradition.* English Literary Studies. Victoria, B.C.: University of Victoria, 1976. Assesses the influence of romance on Fielding's novel, despite his repudiation of romance in favor of history.

Paulson, Ronald, ed. *Fielding: A Collection of Critical Essays.* Twentieth Century Views. Englewood Cliffs, N.J.: Prentice-Hall, 1962. An excellent collection of essays, including contributions by Watt, Empson, Spilka, Mack, Sherburn, and Coolidge.

————. *Satire and the Novel in Eighteenth-Century England.* New Haven: Yale University Press, 1967. Includes a lengthy discussion of Fielding's work (and of *Tom Jones* in particular).

Paulson, Ronald, and Thomas Lockwood, eds. *Henry Fielding: The Critical Heritage.* London: Routledge and Kegan Paul, and Totowa, N.J.: Barnes and Noble, 1969. Valuable collection of eighteenth-century opinions about Fielding, with a good introduction.

Poupard, Dennis, and Mark W. Scott, eds. *Literature Criticism from 1400 to 1800.* Vol. 1. Detroit: Gale Research Co., 1984. Valuable collection of critical views from the age of Fielding to our own day.

Preston, John. *The Created Self: The Reader's Role in Eighteenth-Century Fiction.* London: Heinemann, 1970. Original and valuable treatment of Fielding's strategy for teaching his readers how to read.

Rawson, C. J. *Henry Fielding: A Critical Anthology.* Harmondsworth, Middlesex: Penguin, 1973. An extremely valuable collection of criticism from Fielding's own time to the present.

————. *Henry Fielding and the Augustan Ideal under Stress: "Nature's Dance of Death" and other Studies.* London: Routledge and Kegan Paul, 1972. Explores the theory that the works of Fielding demonstrate "a sense of beleaguered harmony, of forms preserved under stress, of feelings of doom and human defeat ceremoniously rendered."

————, ed. *Henry Fielding.* Profiles in Literature. London: Routledge and Kegan Paul, 1968. Selections with commentary designed to illustrate various features of Fielding's art.

Rogers, Pat. *Henry Fielding.* London: Paul Elek, and New York: Scribner, 1979. Good introduction to Fielding's life and works.

Sacks, Sheldon. *Fiction and the Shape of Belief: A Study of Henry Fielding with Glances at Swift, Johnson, and Richardson.* Chicago, University of

Chicago Press, 1964. Uses Fielding to argue that a novelist's ethical beliefs, opinions, and prejudices are reflected in his work.

Scholes, Robert, and Robert Kellogg. *The Nature of Narrative*. Oxford: Oxford University Press, 1966. Contains a number of suggestive discussions on aspects of Fielding's art.

Sherbo, Arthur. *Studies in the Eighteenth-Century English Novel*. Lansing: Michigan State University Press, 1969. More than half these essays deal with aspects of Fielding's art; of particular interest are those on the narrator in Fielding and the distinction between "inside" and "outside" readers in Fielding's novels.

Shesgreen, Sean. *Literary Portraits in the Novels of Henry Fielding*. DeKalb: Northern Illinois University Press, 1972. Examines the function and methods of characterization in Fielding's novels.

Simpson, K. G., ed. *Henry Fielding: Justice Observed*. London: Vision Press, and Totowa, N. J.: Barnes and Noble, 1985. A useful collection of new essays by modern critics, including Golden, Kinkead-Weekes, Reilly, and Low.

Smallwood, Angela J. *Fielding and the Woman Question: The Novels of Henry Fielding and Feminist Debate, 1700–1750*. Hemel Hempstead: Harvester Wheatsheaf, and New York: St. Martin's Press, 1989. Argues that feminist argument was very much alive in Fielding's lifetime, and must be counted a significant part of the context of his work.

Spearman, Diana. *The Novel and Society*. London: Routledge and Kegan Paul, 1966. Provocative discussion of Fielding that challenges some of the arguments of Ian Watt's *The Rise of the Novel*.

Spector, Robert D., eds. *Essays on the Eighteenth-Century Novel*. Bloomington and London: Indiana University Press, 1965. Includes essays by Kermode, Spilka, and Crane.

Tave, Stuart M. *The Amiable Humorist: A Study in the Comic Theory and Criticism of the Eighteenth and Early Nineteenth Centuries*. Chicago: University of Chicago Press, 1960. Useful background material for Fielding's comic art.

Varey, Simon. *Henry Fielding*. Cambridge: Cambridge University Press, 1986. A very useful study of the life and works of Fielding, with separate chapters on the major texts.

Watt, Ian. *The Rise of the Novel: Studies in Defoe, Richardson and Fielding*. London: Hogarth Press, 1987 (first published by Chatto and Windus, 1957). A seminal work, one of the most important studies of the novel, with indispensable chapters on Fielding.

Williams, Ioan, ed. *Novel and Romance, 1700–1800: A Documentary Record*. London: Routledge and Kegan Paul, 1970. A collection of eighteenth-century statements about the novel form.

Selected Bibliography

Wright, Andrew. *Henry Fielding: Mask and Feast.* Berkeley and Los Angeles: University of California Press, 1965. Stresses the festive role of the fiction in arguing that the novels are more comic than satiric.

Zirker, Malvin R., Jr. *Fielding's Social Pamphlets: A Study of "An Enquiry into the Causes of the Late Increase of Robbers" and "A Proposal for Making an Effectual Provision for the Poor."* Berkeley and Los Angeles: University of California Press, 1966. A study of the legal-sociological writings of Fielding's last years, and an important account of his social outlook, especially as regards crime and the lower classes.

Articles and Chapters of Books

Alter, Robert. "The Picaroon Domesticated." In *Rogue's Progress: Studies in the Picaresque Novel.* Cambridge, Mass.: Harvard University Press, 1964. Examines the ways in which *Tom Jones* deviates from the norms of this literary form.

Baker, Sheridan. "Henry Fielding's Comic Romances." *Papers of the Michigan Academy of Sciences, Arts, and Letters* 45 (1960):411–19. "Romance" is the key word in the preface to *Joseph Andrews*; shows how, in Fielding's later works, the tone of real romance emerges.

Battestin, Martin C. "Fielding's Definition of Wisdom: Some Functions of Ambiguity and Emblem in *Tom Jones.*" *Journal of English Literary History* 35 (1968):188–217. See *Tom Jones* as an exercise in the fictive definition of virtue or moral wisdom, in which "Walking Concepts" act out the meaning of various virtues and vices; the novel is the expression in art of Fielding's Christian vision.

———. "Osborne's *Tom Jones:* Adapting a Classic." *Virginia Quarterly Review* 42 (1966). Reprinted in Compton, *Henry Fielding: Tom Jones, a Casebook.* Interesting analysis of the film based on Fielding's novel.

———. "Tom Jones: The Argument of Design." In *The Augustan Milieu: Essays Presented to Louis A. Landa,* edited by Henry Knight Miller and others, pp. 288–319. Oxford: Clarendon Press, 1970. Sets the novel within a frame of cosmic and social order, conceived in the still compatible terms of Christian humanism and Newtonian science.

Booth, Wayne C. "The Self-Conscious Narrator in Comic Fiction before *Tristram Shandy.*" *PMLA* 67 (1952):163–85. Part of the essay deals with Fielding's use of his first-person narrator.

Chesterton, G. K. "*Tom Jones* and Morality." in *All Things Considered.* New York: John Lane Co., 1918. Humorously paradoxical defense of Tom Jones as a moral character.

Coley, William B. "The Background of Fielding's Laughter." *Journal of*

English Literary History 26, (1959): 229–52. In reaction against an alleged overemphasis of Fielding's moral seriousness, Coley argues that Fielding is above all a comic artist who deliberately trafficked in the "unideal" aspects of life.

Cooke, Arthur L. "Henry Fielding and the Writers of Heroic Romance." *PMLA* 62 (1947):984–94. Despite his very different practice, Fielding's theory of the comic prose epic is strikingly similar to that of Mlle. de Scudéry.

Coolidge, John S. "Fielding and 'Conservation of Character.'" *Modern Philology*, 57, no. 4 (May 1960):245–59. Examines Fielding's development as a novelist by comparing the technical and structural differences between *Tom Jones* and *Amelia*.

Crane, R. S. "The Plot of *Tom Jones*." *Journal of General Education*, 4, no. 2 (January 1950):112–30. A classic example of neo-Aristotelian analysis; Fielding's novel is read as a representation of human experience in which plot unifies the diverse elements of the work in a structure essentially comic.

Davis, Lennard J. *Factual Fictions: The Origins of the English Novel.* New York: Columbia University Press, 1983. Sees the novel as a discourse for reinforcing particular ideologies and as tied to particular power relations; contains a chapter on politics and fact in Fielding.

Dyson, A. E. *The Crazy Fabric: Essays in Irony.* London: Macmillan, and New York: St. Martin's Press, 1965. Contains a valuable chapter on Fielding arguing that he was not a genuine satirist but an essentially comic writer.

Goldknopf, David. "The Failure of Plot in *Tom Jones*." *Criticism* 2 no. 3. (Summer 1969):262–74. Discusses the structurally "denigrating" effects of the interpolations in *Tom Jones*, arguing that Fielding used these narrative devices to mask the triviality of his "banal, romantic comedy."

Greene, Graham. "Fielding and Sterne." In *From Anne to Victoria,* edited by Bonamy Dobrée. London: Cassell, 1937. Reprinted in *The Lost Childhood.* London: Eyre and Spottiswoode, 1951. Acknowledges the importance of Fielding as technical innovator, but hails Sterne as the greater genius.

Hatfield, Glenn W. "The Serpent and the Dove: Fielding's Irony and the Prudence Theme of *Tom Jones*." *Modern Philology* 65 (1967):17–32. Argues that *Tom Jones* is an attempt to reclaim the proper and original moral sense of prudence, to rehabilitate a word that had fallen into disrepute.

Hazlitt, William. "On the English Novelists." In *Lectures on the English Comic Writers.* London: Taylor and Hessey, 1819. Reprinted in *Lectures on the English Comic Writers, with Miscellaneous Essays.* London:

Selected Bibliography

J. M. Dent, 1910. One of the most important critics of the Romantic age praises Fielding for his narrative realism and insight into human nature.

Hilles, Frederick W. "Art and Artifice in *Tom Jones*." In *Imagined Worlds: Essays on some English Novels and Novelists in Honour of John Butt*, edited by Maynard Mack and Ian Gregor. London: Methuen, 1968. Examines the symmetrical arrangement of *Tom Jones* and concludes that the world of the novel is a reflection of a reflection of real life, with a form and structure denied to real life.

Humphreys, A. R., "Fielding's Irony: Its Methods and Effects." *Review of English Studies* 18, no. 70 (April 1942):183–96. Where Swift's irony is mockingly misanthropic, Fielding's is humanistic, attempting to enlighten the reader to the possibility of personal and social improvement.

Hutchens, Eleanor N. "Prudence in *Tom Jones:* A Study of Connotative Irony." *Philological Quarterly* 39 (1960):496–507. Fielding takes the word "prudence," with its normally positive connotations, and puts it in a context in which its literary meaning pertains, but its positive connotations do not (as in calling Blifil's calculation "prudence").

Irwin, W. R. "Satire and Comedy in the Works of Henry Fielding." *Journal of English Literary History*, 13 (1946):168–88. Lists Fielding's particular objects of satiric attack—pedantic critics, bad plays, meddling producers, etc.; then shows how in his theory of the comic prose epic Fielding integrated these into a coherent whole.

Kay, Donald, ed. *A Provision of Human Nature: Essays on Fielding and Others in Honor of Miriam Austin Locke*. Tuscaloosa: University of Alabama Press, 1977. Essays devoted to Fielding's literary theories, ethics, and art. Contributors include Wolfe, Hutchens, and Eaves.

Kermode, Frank. "Richardson and Fielding." *Cambridge Journal* 4 (1950): 106–114. An important essay attacking Fielding as morally simplistic and superficial (reprinted in Spector, *Essays on the Eighteenth-Century Novel*).

Lutwack, Leonard. "Mixed and Uniform Prose Styles in the Novel." *Journal of Aesthetics and Art Criticism* 18(1960):350–57. Contrasts Fielding's and Richardson's styles, the former being characterized by shifts from narrative to essay to drama.

McKeon, Michael. *The Origins of the English Novel 1600–1740*. Baltimore and London: Johns Hopkins University Press, 1987. Discusses the problems associated with current accounts of the rise of the novel, calling attention to Watt's limitations; contains an interesting chapter on *Shamela* and *Joseph Andrews*.

McKillop, Alan Dugald. *The Early Masters of English Fiction*. Lawrence: University of Kansas Press, 1967. Contains a good chapter on Fielding, stressing the author's major themes, intentions, and techniques. Good general introduction.

————. "Some Recent Views of *Tom Jones*." *College English* 21 (1959):17–22. A survey of the interpretations of Crane, Van Ghent, Watt, and others.

Miller, Henry Knight. "Some Functions of Rhetoric in *Tom Jones*." *Philological Quarterly* 45(1966):209–35. Stresses Fielding's consciousness of rhetoric and examines how the typical strategies of rhetoric repeatedly enter the narrative of *Tom Jones*.

Murphy, Arthur. "An Essay on the Life and Genius of Henry Fielding, Esq." (1762). In *The Works of Henry Fielding*, vol. 1, edited by James P. Browne. London: Bickers and Son, H. Sotheran and Co., 1871. The first biography, which was included in the first collected edition of Fielding's works, it helped to establish the popular image of Fielding as a "dissipated rake."

Murry, J. Middleton. "In Defence of Fielding." In *Unprofessional Essays*. London: Jonathan Cape, 1956. A response to Leavis's attack on Fielding in *The Great Tradition* in which Murry vigorously defends *Tom Jones* as a novel exhibiting humanist values.

Park, William. "Fielding and Richardson." *PMLA* 81, no. 5 (October 1966):381–88. Outlines the stock themes, characters, and situations employed by mid-eighteenth-century English novelists and emphasizes the similarities between Fielding's and Richardson's works.

Paulson, Ronald. "Fielding in *Tom Jones:* The Historian, the Poet, and the Mythologist." In *Augustan Worlds: Essays in Honour of A. R. Humphreys*, edited by J. C. Hilson, M. M. B. Jones, and J. R. Watson. Leicester: Leicester University Press, 1978. Relates the Jacobite Rebellion of 1745 to *Tom Jones;* just as false history is the subject of Fielding's *The Jacobite's Journal*, so is it too of his novel—Tom is the true historical figure beneath the Jacobitish myth.

Politi, Jina. *The Novel and Its Presuppositions: Changes in the Conceptual Structure of Novels in the 18th and 19th Centuries.* Amsterdam: Adolf M. Hakkert N. V., 1976. An original and stimulating study in which Politi argues that Fielding's world model in *Tom Jones* displays the operation of law in its universe as it had come to be defined by the science of his day.

Poovey, Mary. " 'Journey from this World to the Next': The Providential Problem in *Clarissa* and *Tom Jones*." In *Eighteenth-Century British Fiction*, edited by Harold Bloom. New York, New Haven, and Philadelphia: Chelsea House Publishers, 1988. An interesting comparison of *Clarissa* and *Tom Jones* as radically opposed artistic expressions of the Christian ethos.

Preston, John. "*Tom Jones* and the Pursuit of True Judgment." *Journal of English Literary History*, 33(1966):315–26. Valuable discussion of Fielding's literary strategies for teaching his reader to be a good judge.

Selected Bibliography

Price, Martin. "Fielding: The Comedy of Forms." In *To the Palace of Wisdom: Studies in Order and Energy from Dryden to Blake*. New York: Doubleday, 1964. Valuable and stimulating discussion of the intellectual background and context of Fielding's art.

Probyn, Clive T. *English Fiction of the Eighteenth Century, 1700–1789*. London and New York: Longman, 1987. Contains an interesting chapter on Fielding's major fiction.

Raleigh, Walter. "Richardson and Fielding." In *The English Novel: A Short Sketch of Its History from the Earliest Times to the Appearance of "Waverley."* London: J. Murray, 1894. Praises *Tom Jones* ("no truer, saner book has ever been written") and Fielding's overall mastery of realistic character portrayal.

Rogers, Katherine M. "Sensitive Feminism vs. Conventional Sympathy: Richardson and Fielding on Women." *Novel: A Forum on Fiction* 9, no. 3 (Spring 1976):256–70. Compares Richardson as a writer sympathetic to women with Fielding as a writer conditioned by the antifeminist prejudices of the time.

Saintsbury, George. "Henry Fielding." *The Bookman* (London) 32, no. 187 (April 1907):7–10. One of the most influential critics at the turn of the century, Saintsbury praises Fielding as a penetrating and honest observer of human behavior and as the most English of English writers.

Scott, Sir Walter. Preface (1820) to *Ballantyne's Novelists' Library*, vol. 1, edited by Walter Scott. London: Hurst, Robinson & Co., 1821. Reprinted as "Fielding" in his *Lives of the Novelists*, pp. 1–28. New York: Oxford University Press, 1906. Calls *Tom Jones* "the first English novel," especially praiseworthy for its truthful characterization.

Sherburn, George. "Fielding's Social Outlook." *Philological Quarterly* 35 (1956):1–23. Reprinted in *Eighteenth-Century English Literature: Modern Essays in Criticism*, edited by James L. Clifford. Oxford: Oxford University Press, 1959. Presents an interesting overall view of Fielding's discrimination between individual and social responsibility.

Shrof, Homai J. *The Eighteenth-Century Novel: The Idea of the Gentleman*. London: Edward Arnold, 1983. Contains a useful chapter on Fielding, arguing that his ideal of good nature is based upon a combination of Shaftesbury and latitudinarian Christianity.

Spacks, Patricia Meyer. "The Dangerous Age." *Eighteenth-Century Studies* 11, no. 4 (Summer 1978):417–38. Examines eighteenth-century attitudes toward the "special social and psychological phenomenon of puberty" as reflected in Fielding's work.

Swann, George R. "Fielding and Empirical Realism." In *Philosophical Parallelism in Six English Novelists: The Conception of Good, Evil and Human Nature*. Philadelphia: University of Pennsylvania Press, 1929.

Analyzes the influence of Shaftesbury and Hume on Fielding's moral thought.

Taine, Hippolyte Adolphe. "Henry Fielding." In *History of English Literature,* vol. 2, translated by Henry Van Laun. London: Colonial Press, 1900. (Originally published as *Histoire de la littérature anglaise,* vol. 3, pp. 424–32. Paris: Librairie de L. Hachette, 1863. Discusses Fielding as an observer of the workings of natural instincts and drives in human beings.

Tavor, Eve. *Scepticism, Society and the Eighteenth-Century Novel.* Basingstoke: Macmillan, 1987. Argues that eighteenth-century novels grew out of the skeptical tradition represented by Locke, Mandeville, and Hume, and regards *Tom Jones* as "epistemological satire."

Thackeray, William Makepeace. "Hogarth, Smollett, and Fielding." In *The English Humourists of the Eighteenth Century.* London: Smith, Elder & Co., 1853; reprinted by Grey Walls Press, 1949. Denigrates *Tom Jones* as likely to encourage immorality, yet admires the novel as a work of literature and Fielding as a masterly portrayer of human nature.

Van Ghent, Dorothy. "On *Tom Jones.*" In *The English Novel: Form and Function.* New York: Holt, Rinehart & Winston, 1953. An important essay that compares *Tom Jones* to a complex architectural figure, "a Palladian palace," a structure radiant and clear. Good on the theme of form and feeling.

West, Rebecca. *The Court and the Castle: A Study of the Interactions of Political and Religious Ideas in Imaginative Literature.* London: Macmillan, 1958, and New Haven: Yale University Press, 1958. Contains an interesting essay on the moral and political background of Fielding's work, concluding that he is "The Great Optimist."

Work, James A. "Henry Fielding, Christian Censor." In *The Age of Johnson: Essays Presented to Chauncey Brewster Tinker,* edited by Frederick W. Hilles. New Haven: Yale University Press, 1949. Calls Fielding "the most important Christian moralist of his generation" and contends that Christian ideology is the underlying impetus behind Fielding's writing.

Bibliographies

Battestin, Martin C. Henry Fielding section of *The New Cambridge Bibliography of English Literature,* vol. 2, edited by George Watson, pp. 925–48. Cambridge: Cambridge University Press, 1971.

Hahn, H. George. *Henry Fielding: An Annotated Bibliography.* Scarecrow Author Bibliographies, no. 41. Metuchen, N.J., and London: Scarecrow Press, 1979.

Morrissey, L. J. *Henry Fielding: A Reference Guide,* edited by Arthur

Selected Bibliography

Weitzman. Boston: G. K. Hall & Co., 1980. Extensive annotated bibliography of works written by and about Fielding from 1755 to 1977, with an introduction that traces the direction of Fielding biographies and criticism.

Stoler, John A., and Richard D. Fulton. *Henry Fielding: An Annotated Bibliography of Twentieth-Century Criticism, 1900–1977.* New York and London: Garland, 1980.

Index

Index

Index

Index

The Author

Patrick Reilly was born in Glasgow and was educated at the University of Glasgow and at Pembroke College, Oxford, where he earned his B.Litt. with the thesis "Jonathan Swift and Seventeenth-Century Scepticism." After a year as a school teacher, Reilly joined the staff of the English Department at the University of Glasgow as assistant lecturer in 1964 and is now reader. His publications include *Jonathan Swift: The Brave Desponder* (1982). *George Orwell: The Age's Adversary* (1986), and *The Literature of Guilt: From "Gulliver" to Golding* (1988), which has separate chapters on Swift. Conrad, Thomas Mann, Orwell, Camus, and William Golding. *Nineteen Eighty-four: Past, Present, and Future* appeared in 1989 as an addition to the list of Twayne's Masterwork Studies. Reilly has also published articles on Orwell, Joyce, Scottish literature, and education and religion and has contributed to several books, including *Henry Fielding: Justice Observed,* edited by K. G. Simpson (1985), and *Modern Scottish Catholicism 1878–1978*, edited by David McRoberts (1979), as well as to four volumes of anthologized literary criticism.